United States Presidents

RICHARD M. NIXON
Revised Edition

Michael A. Schuman

 Enslow Publishers, Inc.
40 Industrial Road   PO Box 38
Box 398   Aldershot
Berkeley Heights, NJ 07922 Hants GU12 6BP
USA   UK
http://www.enslow.com

To my siblings, Richard, Sybil, and in memory of Larry.

Library of Congress Cataloging–in–Publication Data

Schuman, Michael.
    Richard M. Nixon / Michael A. Schuman.— Rev. ed.
      p. cm. — (United States presidents)
    Summary: Traces the life of the thirty-seventh president, discussing his childhood in California, careers in law and the military, his terms as vice president and president, his comeback following the Watergate scandal, and roles as political consultant and elder statesman.
    Includes bibliographical references (p.) and index.
    ISBN 0-7660-2031-2
    1. Nixon, Richard M. (Richard Milhous), 1913–1994—Juvenile literature. 2. Presidents—United States—Biography—Juvenile literature. [1. Nixon, Richard M. (Richard Milhous), 1913–1994. 2. Presidents.] I. Title. II. Series.
E856.S29   2003
973.924'092—dc21
                           2002155530

Illustration Credits: Dwight D. Eisenhower Library, pp. 58, 60; National Archives and Records Administration, pp. 10, 70, 72; The Richard Nixon Library & Birthplace, p. 4; Richard Nixon Library Collections, pp. 14, 38, 48, 55, 101, 103; Whittier College, pp. 12, 16, 20, 25, 27, 29, 32.

Source Document Credits: National Archives, p. 91; Richard Nixon Library Collections, pp. 36, 45, 47, 52, 68, 69, 79; Whittier College, p. 24.

Cover Illustration: Background & Portrait: The Richard Nixon Library & Birthplace.

Contents

Richard Nixon

1

BREAKING DOWN
THE WALL

In February 1972, President Richard M. Nixon stepped off an airplane in the city of Peking, China (now called Beijing). As president, he had made many trips before. However, this one was very different.

No American had officially visited mainland China for nearly twenty-five years. Officially, Americans had not even spoken with the Chinese leaders in all that time. China continued to be totally ignored by American statesmen. It was as if China was located on the other side of the moon.

Yet China is a very important nation. There are more people living there than in any other country in the world. China also has, as it did then, the ability to make nuclear weapons. Nuclear weapons are the most dangerous weapons on earth. One nuclear bomb is capable of destroying an entire city.

Why had the United States and China ignored each other for so long? There are several reasons.

Mainland China (officially called the People's Republic of China) and the United States have different forms of government. The United States is a democratic capitalist country. That means that most businesses are owned collectively by private persons or companies. China is a Communist country. In pure communism, all businesses are owned collectively by the community (all the citizens of a country). There is no private business.

In Chinese communism, all businesses are owned by the government. The only official political party is the Communist party. There is no tolerance for people with differing views. Chinese citizens who openly criticized their government were punished. Many Americans were scared that Communist countries like China would try to force their type of government on the United States. For years Americans thought there was no good reason even to talk with any nation that practiced communism in any form.

Most of China sits on the mainland of Asia. Off its coast is the island of Taiwan. Taiwan is also part of China. However, it has never been Communist. So Taiwan had diplomatic relations with the United States whereas Communist China did not.

William Rogers was Nixon's secretary of state. The secretary of state oversees relations with foreign countries. Rogers later explained other reasons why China was isolated at the time. He noted:

> One reason is distance. It's a long way from the United States, but it is also a real distance from the United States in terms of culture. It's made up of a lot of different groups. We might call them tribal groups. Over the years they have had many, many conflicts among themselves. Then they formed support for the communist idea of government. So these two factors really made it isolated from our standpoint.[1]

Nixon believed things needed to change. In 1969, Nixon began studying the prospects of opening relations with China. Rogers explained:

> I think they each [the United States and China] thought it was going to be mutually beneficial. First, I think they thought it might contribute to peace in the world. Two countries with different philosophies of government might continue to have their relationship deteriorate. Therefore it would be better to get to know each other a little bit. Secondly, the world had changed to the point where there was a lot more trade with each other . . . so each side thought it would be beneficial from a standpoint of peace and a standpoint of trade.[2]

People suspected that there was one additional reason that Nixon went to China. One other very powerful nation at the time was the Union of Soviet Socialist Republics (also known as the USSR, or Soviet Union). The USSR consisted of Russia and fourteen other smaller republics. Today some of these republics are separate nations.

Back then, the USSR was a Communist nation like China. Many Americans feared the USSR as much as they did China. However, even though both the USSR and China were Communist nations, they were not friends. They were strong enemies and feared each other. Nixon and his staff figured, what better way to hurt an enemy like the USSR than to make friends with its enemy?

When Nixon announced that he would visit China in 1972, Americans were stunned. Most people supported the idea. However, some were troubled by it.

Many Americans were concerned that a visit to Communist China might hurt relations with Taiwan, a friend of the United States. Others still did not want to deal at all with any Communist country.

Nixon insisted that he was doing the right thing. He said, "We must recognize that the government of the People's Republic of China and the government of the United States have had great differences. We will have differences in the future. But what we must do is to find a way to see that we can have differences without being enemies in war."[3]

In many ways, Nixon seemed the least likely president to make this trip. As a politician, he had worked hard since the 1940s to fight the spread of communism. It was a surprise to some that he would be the president who would try to open relations with Communist China.

George McGovern was the Democratic candidate who ran for president against Nixon in 1972. McGovern said, "Some of my colleagues used to quip that Nixon could do it [go to China] because he didn't have

Nixon to worry about. He was the symbol of the hard line anti-communist position that for many years had opposed any kind of opening to . . . China."[4]

When Nixon landed at the Peking airport, he was greeted by Premier Chou En-lai of China. The Chinese and American national anthems were played. Everyone wondered if and when Nixon would meet Mao Tse-tung, chairman of the Chinese Communist party. Although Chou En-lai's title was premier, Mao was the true leader of the nation. To everyone's surprise, Nixon and Mao met just hours later. The two leaders had a friendly discussion.

Nixon and Chou En-lai spent part of the next few days in meetings. They went to cultural events together. The two leaders attended formal banquets. They toured China and saw the huge country's many interesting sights.

Perhaps the most famous Chinese landmark is the Great Wall of China. This stone wall runs for about four thousand miles across northern China.[5] Work on it began about 214 B.C. The wall is so huge that it is the only man-made structure on earth that astronauts have been able to see from outer space.

After visiting the Great Wall, Nixon said he hoped that "walls will not divide peoples of the world, that peoples regardless of differences in philosophy and background will have an opportunity to communicate with each other and know each other."[6]

Nixon returned home after eight days. No major

The Nixons visit the Great Wall on February 24, 1972, during their trip to China.

treaties were signed on the trip. However, just the fact that the leaders had met helped break down a giant wall separating two powerful countries.

William Rogers later said that the trip "made the world a safer place. We are having diplomatic relations with China, and large amounts of trade and an exchange of people—a lot of Americans go there and a lot of Chinese come here. All those things contribute to world peace, more understanding."[7]

Nixon as a baby.

2

I Want to Work
on the Railroad

R ichard Milhous Nixon was born on January 9, 1913, in Yorba Linda, California. Yorba Linda is in the southern part of the state, about thirty-five miles from downtown Los Angeles.

Today when people think of southern California, images of movie stars, busy freeways, and skate-boarders by the beach might pop into their minds. But southern California when Richard Nixon was a child was not at all like it is today.

Most movies then were made in New York. The first movie studio in Los Angeles did not open until 1911.[1] There were no freeways. In fact, there were few roads. Cars were new and many people still got around by horse and carriage.

Yorba Linda was a small farming village where most

residents raised citrus fruit for a living. Orange trees grew wild in groves that today are occupied by shopping malls, houses, and businesses. Nixon's father, Francis Anthony "Frank" Nixon, was trying to earn a living as a citrus farmer.

Richard Nixon was born in his parents' bedroom in a five-room house built by his father. That day the weather was about as cold as it gets in southern California. Temperatures at night had dipped into the mid-twenties.

The Nixons' family doctor lived about twelve miles away in another small town, called Whittier. He drove

This is the home built by Nixon's father, Frank, where Richard was born and spent his early years.

to Yorba Linda in a horse and buggy to deliver the baby. Because it was so cold, the baby was wrapped in a blanket and placed in a laundry basket to keep warm.

Richard Milhous Nixon was the Nixons' second child. He had an older brother named Harold. Richard was named in honor of King Richard the Lionhearted, who ruled England from 1189 to 1199. His middle name, Milhous, was his mother's maiden name. Nixon's mother, Hannah Milhous Nixon, was fascinated with English history. She loved it so much that she named all but one of her five children after English kings.

Frank and Hannah Nixon belonged to a religious group called the Society of Friends, also known as Quakers. Quakers are pacifists. This means that they reject all forms of violence, especially war. Before moving to Yorba Linda, Frank and Hannah lived in Whittier, a community in which most residents were Quakers.

Almost two years after Richard was born, Hannah Nixon had another baby. He was named Francis Donald, after his father.

Times were tough for the Nixons. The little house the Nixons called home had no indoor plumbing. Instead, there was an outhouse in the backyard. All three boys slept in one small upstairs bedroom. Then in 1918, Hannah gave birth to a fourth son, Arthur. Now four boys shared the cramped bedroom.

Nixon later recalled, "It was crowded. We sometimes had arguments. But except for occasional pillow fights, we got along famously."[2]

Nixon (right) is shown here with his parents and brothers Harold (left) and Donald in 1918.

Richard was not a fun-loving child. His first teacher, Mary George, thought he was unusual compared with his classmates. She recalled, "He was a very solemn child and rarely ever smiled or laughed. I have no recollection of him playing with others in the playground, which undoubtedly he did. . . ."[3] His classmates soon gave him the nickname "Gloomy Gus."

George also remembered that Richard was very smart. "He absorbed knowledge of any kind like a blotter," she later said.[4] From a very early age, Richard loved to read. His favorite magazine was *National Geographic*.[5] He said, "I would spend hours seeing the world from our living room. . . ."[6]

Richard had other adventures on his mind. There were railroad tracks within a mile of his house. Engines from the Santa Fe Railroad traveled them daily. A railroad engineer named Everett Barnum was a family friend. Barnum often told the boys romantic stories about railroad life. Nixon said, "As a young boy in Yorba Linda . . . my goal was to become a railroad engineer. Sometimes at night I was awakened by the sound of a train whistle, and I would dream of the far-off places I wanted to visit someday."[7]

When not dreaming of faraway places, Richard could often be found playing the piano in the living room. An uncle began giving him lessons at age seven, and he became a skilled musician. He soon was playing other instruments, too, including the violin, clarinet, accordion, and saxophone.

Nixon later commented, "I have often thought that if there had been a good rap group around in those days, I might have chosen a career in music instead of politics."[8]

As Richard was growing up, his father was finding it more and more difficult to earn a living as a farmer. So when Richard was nine, Frank Nixon decided to change careers. He moved his family to East Whittier. There he ran a combined grocery store and gas station.

Keeping the store running was a full-family effort. Everyone who was old enough did his or her part. Although he was only nine, Richard woke up at four o'clock in the morning to travel with his father to Los Angeles. There they bought produce at a large vegetable market. Father and son brought it back to the Nixon store where Richard would wash and display it.

Richard then caught a school bus at eight o'clock. After a day in school he came home and worked in the store again. Finally, he did his homework and went to bed. Richard slept only about four hours a night.[9]

In spite of this punishing schedule, Richard remained a top student. He continued to show a gift for music. Because of that talent, his parents had him transfer to another school when he was in the seventh grade. It was in the town of Lindsay, about two hundred miles north of East Whittier. There Richard would live with his uncle and aunt, Harold and Jane Beeson. Jane Beeson was a professional music teacher.

Richard's piano playing improved, but he was

homesick for his parents and brothers. Also, the Beesons were much stricter than his parents. After five months, Richard moved back home.

Shortly after Richard returned, his little brother Arthur became gravely sick. Arthur was just seven years old. Doctors came to visit Arthur and perform some tests on him. The tests brought bad news. Richard remembered his father coming down the stairs with tears on his face. Frank Nixon said, "The doctors are afraid that the little darling is going to die."[10] It was the first time Richard had ever seen his father cry.[11]

Arthur died on August 19, 1925. The doctors said he died from either tubercular meningitis or encephalitis. Both are diseases that affect the brain. Richard wrote, "For weeks after Arthur's funeral, there was not a day that I did not think about him and cry."[12]

Hannah Nixon later said, "It was Arthur's passing which first stirred within Richard a determination to help make up for our loss, by making us very proud of him."[13]

In the autumn of 1926, Richard entered high school. As in grammar school, he was an excellent student. However, he still was not popular. He was a shy, serious boy. Today kids might call someone like him a nerd. At times he was picked on and made fun of. He decided to get back at those who picked on him. He did it not by revenge but by success.

As an adult, Nixon remembered what made him want to succeed. "What starts the process really are laughs and slights and snubs when you are a kid.

The Nixon boys pose with the family dog in 1922. From the left: Harold, Richard, Arthur, and Donald.

Sometimes it's because you're poor or Irish or Jewish or Catholic or ugly or simply that you are skinny. But if you are reasonably intelligent and if your anger is deep enough and strong enough you learn that you can change those attitudes by excellence, personal gut performance, while those who have everything are sitting on their fat butts."[14]

Nixon became a star on his school debate team. He led the team to regional and state championships. He took up acting at school and had a girlfriend. Her name was Ola Florence Welch. One time he performed with her on stage for the school's Latin Club. The play was called *Aeneid,* based on a poem written by Virgil, a poet of ancient Rome. Years later, Nixon remembered an embarrassing moment.

At one point in the play he had to wrap his arms around Ola. He recalled, "I'll never forget . . . [we heard] the hoots and the catcalls and the whistles from all the kids out there [in the audience]. We both turned red. . . ."[15]

As a senior in high school, Richard ran for school president against a member of the junior class. He was strongly favored to win until a third student named Robert Logue entered the race. Logue was a handsome young man who played on both the football and basketball teams of the high school. Whereas Nixon was quiet and studious, Logue was outgoing and charming. Logue won the election in a landslide. It was Nixon's first run for office.

As his high school years were coming to an end, Nixon was recruited by two of the best universities in the country. One was Harvard University in Cambridge, Massachusetts. The other was Yale University in New Haven, Connecticut. It seemed that Nixon's future was bright. However, there were serious problems occurring in his family.

Richard's older brother, Harold, was very sick. He suffered from tuberculosis, a disease that affects the lungs. Today it can be detected early and treated. That was not so in 1930. The Nixons spent a great amount of money on medical care for Harold.

Both of Richard's scholarships would have paid for his tuition, which is the cost of college classes. But the scholarships did not cover living expenses such as food and lodging. They also did not cover the cost of traveling from California to the East Coast.[16] There was no way the Nixons could afford to pay these costs.

There was one other change in the Nixon household. Another baby was born in May 1930. He was the Nixons' fifth son and was named Edward. Much of Frank and Hannah Nixon's attention was devoted to Harold and to baby Edward. Richard knew his parents needed his help in their store.

Richard Nixon said good-bye to any chance of an education at an Ivy League school. He decided to live at home and attend the much smaller Whittier College.[17] In September 1930, he went to his first college class.

3

Marriage, War, and No Dancing

At college, Nixon was as active as ever. He joined the debate team, the glee club, and the drama club. He was elected to the student council and made the freshman football team. All the while, he continued to help out with the family grocery store.

Nixon greatly admired his football coach, Wallace Newman. Newman was an American Indian known by the nickname "Chief." Nixon remembered that Newman "had no tolerance for the view that how you play the game counts more than whether you win or lose. He believed in always playing cleanly . . . but he used to say, 'Show me a good loser, and I'll show you a loser.' He also said, 'When you lose, get mad—but get mad at yourself, not at your opponent.'"[1]

Nixon got high grades in his classes, just as he had

Nixon acted in many plays while at Whittier College. This program shows he is cast as Thomas Greenleaf in a play called Bird in Hand.

in high school. He also continued dating Ola Florence Welch, who was a student at Whittier, too. Yet for all his activity on campus, Nixon was still a very serious young man. A friend confessed that "he didn't seem to have a sense of fun."[2]

Whittier College did not have fraternities. Instead, it had a club of male students called a "student society." The student society was named the Franklins. Members of the Franklins were from wealthy backgrounds. Because Nixon was from a poor family, he was not asked to join the Franklins.

Instead of taking rejection quietly, Nixon and a friend named Dean Triggs created another student

Nixon with his girlfriend, Ola Florence Welch.

society. It would be a rival to the Franklins. Nixon and Triggs called their club the Orthogonians. The name has a complex background. It comes from the word *orthogonal*, meaning something composed of right angles, or square-shaped. Nixon and Triggs considered themselves to be "square shooters" or honest and straightforward men.

During that time, there was more sad news in Nixon's family. Brother Harold died in March 1933 from tuberculosis. Nixon was deeply saddened.[3] However, he did not have much time to dwell on the event. Just two months after Harold's death was the election for president of the Whittier student body. Nixon was running as a representative of the Orthogonians. A popular student named Dick Thomson ran representing the Franklins. Based on popularity, Thomson should have won the election.

Nixon made a bold campaign promise. Whittier was a Quaker college and, therefore, had strict rules governing campus life. In the 1930s it was common for religious schools to see dancing as sinful. At Whittier, formal dances were not allowed.

Nixon promised he would work to have dances allowed on campus. He won the election and officially became class president in September 1933. It was the beginning of his senior year.

The new president went to work on fulfilling his election promise. He spoke to the college's governing body. He told the board members that students were

Nixon as he looked when he attended Whittier College.

going to dance anyway. He suggested that it would be better for students to dance on campus where they could be supervised.

The board was persuaded. The ban on dancing was lifted. Dances could now take place, though the word *dance* was never actually used. These events were officially called "large social affairs."[4] This was Nixon's first success at policy making.

It is interesting to note that Frank and Hannah Nixon were at odds with their son on this issue. As religious Quakers, they were in favor of keeping the ban. Another striking fact is that Nixon did not like to dance and was regarded by classmates as a poor dancer.

Nixon graduated from Whittier College in May 1934. He was ranked the third best student in a class of eighty-five graduates.[5]

At about that time he saw an inviting notice on a campus bulletin board. It was an announcement that Duke University in North Carolina was offering scholarships for its School of Law. Nixon applied and was awarded one. Things seemed to be working out in his life. He and Ola continued dating happily and began saving money for an engagement ring.

Nixon moved to North Carolina and started attending classes at Duke in September 1934. He and Ola regularly wrote love letters to each other.

For the most part, times were tough for people in the 1930s. The period from 1929 to 1939 is known as the Great Depression. In 1932, more than 12 million

Americans, or about 10 percent of the population, were out of work.[6] Many who had jobs were struggling. Money was hard to come by.

Nixon was always low on food and seemed to live on a diet of candy bars. He remembered, "For three years . . . I had a Milky Way for breakfast. . . . And it did damage to my teeth, but it certainly was good for the pocketbook because it only cost five cents."[7]

Nixon returned home to California during the summer of 1935. He continued to see Ola, but he learned she was also seeing someone else. His name was Gail Jobe. Jobe was good-looking and loved to take Ola dancing.

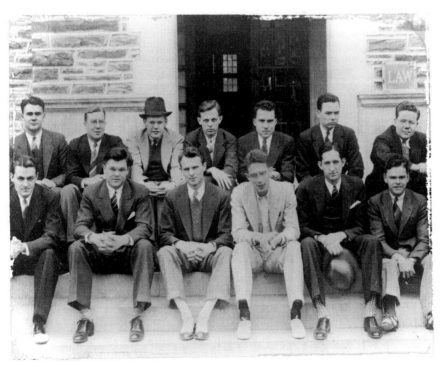

Nixon (top row, third from right) appears here with fellow members of the Duke Law School Honor Society.

In September, Nixon returned to law school. He regularly wrote letters to Ola. However, she began to fall deeper and deeper in love with Gail Jobe. In December, she wrote Nixon and told him she was going to marry Jobe. Ola returned the money that they had been saving for an engagement ring. Yet Nixon refused to give up. He still wrote to her. She wrote back and asked him to stop writing. But he continued to write to her until just a few weeks before the wedding.

Finally, Nixon gave up. He sent Ola and Jobe a wedding present and a warm letter wishing them good luck. Ola later explained that Nixon was too serious for her to marry him.[8]

Nixon began preparing for graduation from law school. However, students cannot practice law simply by graduating from law school. They have to pass a difficult test called the bar examination. Nixon passed it in mid-1937.

Nixon hoped to find work with a big New York City law firm, but was unsuccessful. He then applied for a job as a lawyer with the Federal Bureau of Investigation (FBI). However, its budget had been cut, making the agency unable to hire more people.

Finally, Nixon moved back to California to look for work. He found a job with a Whittier law firm named Wingert and Bewley. At first he handled mostly divorce cases. After a while, he became the chief trial lawyer in his law firm.

One of Nixon's fellow lawyers was named Wallace

Black. Black enjoyed acting in a local theater group. One time Black was too busy to play a role he had studied for. He asked Nixon to take over for him. Nixon did and found that he still enjoyed acting.

On January 16, 1938, he went to the theater to audition for a part in a mystery titled *The Dark Tower*. Also trying out for a part was a high-school teacher named Patricia Ryan. She was pretty, with long, wavy red hair.

For Dick Nixon, it was love at first sight. He went up to her and said, "I think we should go out because I'm going to marry you some day."[9]

At first Pat was cool toward Nixon. But he continued to pursue her, and before long they were going out regularly. Their dates consisted of walks on the beach, music concerts, and movies.

Patricia Ryan's real name was Thelma Catherine Ryan. She was born on March 16, 1912. Because she was born just a few hours before St. Patrick's Day (March 17), her parents called her Pat. By the time she was eighteen, both of her parents had died. Since she had always been called Pat at home, she officially changed her name to Patricia.[10]

In March 1940, Dick drove Pat to Dana Point, a high bluff overlooking the Pacific Ocean. It is a romantic spot, and the sun was setting. Nixon proposed marriage and Pat accepted. They were married on June 21, 1940, and took a two-week honeymoon to Mexico. Upon returning, they moved into a small apartment.

Life at home was cozy and comfortable, but

This was Nixon's favorite photo of his wife, Pat.

overseas, there was scary news. War was raging in Europe and in the Far East. In Europe, the major aggressor countries were Germany and Italy. Germany had invaded and was occupying much of Europe. In Asia, the invading country was Japan. Japan was controlling a great part of eastern Asia. Americans wondered if and when the United States would become involved in the war.

At that time, Nixon received an opportunity to take a job in Washington, D.C., in the government's Office of Price Administration (OPA). The OPA's job was to help control prices of goods. The OPA needed lawyers, and the Nixons were eager to live somewhere new. He was hired and was to start work in January 1942.

On Sunday, December 7, 1941, Japan bombed the United States naval base at Pearl Harbor, Hawaii. The next day, United States president Franklin Roosevelt asked Congress to declare war against Japan. Congress did so. Days later, Germany declared war on the United States. The United States was now fully involved in World War II.

Just over a month after the Pearl Harbor attack, Nixon began work at the OPA in Washington. In August 1942, Nixon enlisted in the Navy. He said he felt it was a responsibility. Pat later said, "I would have felt mighty uncomfortable if Dick hadn't done his part."[11]

Nixon's Quaker parents were troubled. Fighting in a war went against their religious beliefs. Nixon later explained, "The problem with Quaker pacifism . . . was that it could only work if one were fighting a civilized, compassionate enemy."[12]

Nixon was sent to the South Pacific. Pat stayed behind. His job as a lawyer allowed him to enter the Navy as a full-fledged lieutenant. Nixon was assigned to a military unit called South Pacific Combat Air Transport Command (SCAT). In the stifling jungles of various islands, he helped direct the movement of military men. He was never involved in any direct fighting, but there were tense moments. In January 1944, he arrived on an island called Bougainville, where Japanese sniper attacks and bombing raids were constant threats.

Though still in the Navy, Nixon was sent back to the United States in August 1944. He served at posts on both the east and west coasts. He was at work at a Navy legal unit in New York City on August 14, 1945, when he learned that Japan had surrendered to the United States. The war was over. Nixon was transferred to the city of Baltimore, Maryland, where he received a letter that would change his life.

4

THE RED FIGHTER

The letter was from a family friend named Herman Perry, a leading Republican in Whittier. Nixon opened the envelope and read the following:

> Dear Dick:
>
> I am writing you this short note to ask if you would like to be a candidate for Congress on the Republican ticket in 1946.
>
> Jerry Voorhis expects to run—registration is about 50-50. The Republicans are gaining.
>
> Please airmail me your reply if you are interested.
>
> Yours very truly, H. L. Perry
>
> P. S. Are you a registered voter in California?[1]

Nixon knew that Democrat Jerry Voorhis had won five straight terms in Congress. However, he also knew that President Harry S. Truman, a Democrat, was not currently popular.

After the war ended, there were shortages of many items, including food and houses. Many blamed the Democrats in office.

Nixon decided to accept Perry's offer and run for Congress in his district. He moved back to California and earned the Republican nomination. Next, he had to beat Voorhis.

In the Nixon household, there was some other exciting news. Pat Nixon gave birth to a daughter on

SOURCE DOCUMENT

AMERICA NEEDS NEW LEADERSHIP NOW!

Elect

RICHARD M. **NIXON**

WORLD WAR II VETERAN

YOUR CONGRESSMAN

A campaign poster for Nixon's successful run for California congressman in 1946.

February 21, 1946. She was named Patricia, but would always be called Tricia.

Away from home, the new father hit the campaign trail. There was another major political issue aside from the shortages. During World War II, both the massive Soviet Union (USSR) and the United States had Germany as a common enemy. So both fought against Germany. This was in spite of the fact that the USSR was a Communist country.

Now the war was over. Americans again felt they had much to fear from this Communist giant.

At the time, the eight nations that made up Eastern Europe had Communist governments. These included Poland, Hungary, Czechoslovakia, Rumania, Bulgaria, Albania, and East Germany. The Soviet Union had direct influence over this group of countries, together known as the Communist bloc. (The eighth nation, Yugoslavia, was also Communist, but it was not directly aligned with the Soviet Union.)

These nations had become Communist soon after World War II was over. As the war wound down, the Americans who had liberated Western Europe were occupying the countries there. The USSR had liberated Eastern Europe and was occupying those nations. An agreement between President Roosevelt and USSR leader Josef Stalin called for free elections in the Eastern European countries the USSR was occupying. However, Stalin went back on his word. He never

The Nixons with their baby daughter Tricia enjoy the front yard of their home in Whittier.

allowed free elections, and the Eastern European nations remained under Communist leadership.

Because of this, many Americans became frightened that the USSR wanted to spread communism into other countries, including the United States. Many believed the Soviets would try to attack the United States. Since no physical fighting took place directly between the two superpowers, this tension between the United States and the Soviet Union was called the Cold War.

It is not hard to see why Americans were fearful. World War II was fresh in everyone's memory. It seemed to some that the USSR was trying to control other countries, just as Germany and Japan had.

Some Americans even distrusted other Americans. They feared that some agreed with the USSR about the Communist form of government and would support the Soviet Union if it ever attacked the United States. Rumors floated around that Communists were working in the American government.

Communists were nicknamed "reds." Persons who were not officially Communists but who sympathized with them were called "pink" or "pinkos." Jerry Voorhis was a liberal Democrat. That means he believed that the federal government should have a large role in making public policy. Some political opponents began to take advantage of people's fears; they publicly called Voorhis red or pink because of his liberal views.

Conservative Republicans are the opposite of liberal Democrats. In general, Republicans believe the federal government should have as small a role as possible in people's lives. They say that companies cannot compete fairly if the government regulates too strongly how they conduct business.

In 1946, many Republicans, including Nixon, attacked Democratic opponents by charging that they agreed with Communist views. Some of the charges were true. Others were not. Some were exaggerations. In Voorhis's case, most charges were exaggerations. Voorhis did belong to liberal political groups. But none was a Communist organization.[2]

In a debate on September 13, 1946, Nixon hammered Voorhis. He accused Voorhis of accepting support from at least one Communist political group.[3] Voorhis fumbled as he answered the charges. In four more debates, Nixon kept up the pressure. Voorhis continued to stumble as he tried to respond to Nixon's charges. Voorhis seemed weak and unsure of his views.

In November, Nixon won a commanding victory. He received more than 57 percent of the total vote.[4] Across the country, the Republicans earned control of both the House of Representatives and the Senate.

Years later, Voorhis said, "All the stops were pulled and Mr. Nixon beat me. He was a good debater. He was a clever debater . . . but I still feel there were a good many below-the-belt blows struck in the campaign."[5]

Nixon himself later commented on his tactics. He said to one of Voorhis's aides, "Of course I knew Jerry Voorhis wasn't a Communist, but I had to win. That's the thing you don't understand. The important thing is to win."[6]

Perhaps the words of his old friend and coach, Chief Newman, were still in Nixon's mind. Newman had always stressed that winning was most important. But Newman also urged his players to play fairly. Did Nixon play fairly?

As might be expected, Representative Nixon supported conservative Republican views on issues of the day. One of these was called the Taft-Hartley bill. It was sponsored by two conservative Republicans: Representative

Fred Hartley, Jr., from New Jersey and an Ohio senator, Robert Taft (the son of President William Howard Taft).

The Taft-Hartley bill would decrease the power of labor unions. In April 1947, Nixon met with another young congressperson to debate the Taft-Hartley bill. He was John F. (Jack) Kennedy, a Democrat from Massachusetts. Kennedy was from a wealthy family and had attended Harvard University.

Nixon supported the bill. Kennedy said there was some good in it. However, he worried that it was too extreme and would start a war between labor and management.[7] The Taft-Hartley bill passed and was voted into law by the Republican-dominated Congress.

Although Kennedy and Nixon were very different and from opposing parties, they had a mutual respect for each other. Historian Christopher Matthews later said, "They became very friendly. I think the only way I can describe it is that Richard Nixon was the smart kid in the class and Kennedy was the cool kid in the class."[8]

Meanwhile, the fear of communism did not let up. One congressional committee was called the House Committee on UnAmerican Activities (HUAC). Its purpose was to find persons or groups who promoted ideas considered to be threatening to the security of the United States. Most of the time, this meant Communists or Communist sympathizers.

HUAC investigated liberal organizations such as peace groups and labor unions. In 1947, HUAC made a special effort to look for Communists working in the movie industry and in the United States government. Soon after taking office, Richard Nixon was appointed to HUAC.

The summer of 1948 was a busy time for the Nixons. On July 5, Pat Nixon gave birth to another girl, whom they named Julie. Less than a month later, Richard Nixon became involved in a spy case that is still being debated to this day.

Besides Nixon, there were two main figures involved in the case. One was Alger Hiss, a handsome and highly respected government official. The other was named Whittaker Chambers, a short, pudgy, rumpled man. He was an editor for *Time* magazine who admitted that he had once been a spy for the Soviet Union.

On August 3, 1948, Chambers was called to testify under oath before HUAC. That meant that he had to swear to answer honestly all questions asked by the committee. In doing so, Chambers gave names of noted persons he said were Communists. The most famous name he reported was Alger Hiss.

Americans were stunned. Hiss was admired for his years of government service. He had worked closely with Presidents Franklin Roosevelt and Harry S. Truman. He had helped organize the founding of the United Nations. Now he was being called a traitor.

Of all the members of HUAC, it was Nixon who seized control of the case. Under oath, Hiss said that Chambers was lying. Hiss said he had never been a Communist and did not sympathize with Communists.

However, Nixon did not trust Hiss. He made it his mission to prove that Hiss was lying.

The case dragged on through 1948. No evidence proving Hiss a Communist was discovered. The stress of the case was taking a toll on Nixon's health. He had trouble sleeping.[9]

In November 1948, President Truman was up for reelection. He won a surprising victory. In addition, the Democrats took back control of the Senate and House of Representatives. There was a chance the Democrats might abolish HUAC. Many Democrats thought HUAC was out to get not only Communists, but also anyone with liberal views. If HUAC was done away with, the case against Hiss would fall apart.

To escape the stress, the Nixons planned a vacation cruise to the Caribbean. They left on December 2. While at sea, Nixon received a telegraph message from another man who was also working on the Hiss case. The message said that written evidence against Hiss had been found. Nixon then received a second message asking him to come home. He left the boat by a seaplane that had been sent by the U.S. Coast Guard, and was flown back to the United States.

Nixon learned that on December 2, two HUAC staff members had visited Chambers at his farm in Maryland. Chambers told them that he had documents proving Hiss was a spy. These were official government documents that Hiss had copied. Some were top secret.

According to Chambers, Hiss copied these papers to give secret information to a Communist nation.

Chambers copied the papers onto microfilm and stored them in a hollowed-out pumpkin in a pumpkin patch on his farm. Some of the papers were in Hiss's handwriting. Documents that were typed matched the exact printing from Hiss's typewriter.

There was now enough evidence to put Hiss on trial. Too much time had passed to legally charge Hiss with espionage (spying for another country). Instead he was charged with perjury (lying under oath).

Hiss continued to claim he was innocent. He said in court, "Until the day I die, I shall wonder how Whittaker Chambers got into my house to use my typewriter."[10]

The trial began on May 31, 1949. It ended on July 8. Of the twelve jurors, eight voted that Hiss was guilty. The other four said Hiss was innocent. A jury with a split decision is called a hung jury. A hung jury cannot deliver a verdict, so a second trial began on November 17, 1949.

The Hiss case was not the only important news story in 1949. A civil war was taking place in China. Communist Chinese were fighting non-Communist (or nationalist) Chinese for control of the country. By autumn, it was clear that the Communists had won control of the country. Now two of the world's biggest countries, the Soviet Union and China, were Communist.

At the same time, the Soviet Union tested an atomic bomb. The atomic bomb is a weapon capable of destroying at least an entire city. The United States had dropped two atomic bombs on Japan to end World War II four years earlier. Americans felt safe knowing the United States was the only country able to build an atomic bomb—that is, until the USSR's atomic test was successful. Americans became even more fearful.

Thanks to his pursuit of Hiss, Nixon was well known as a strong anti-Communist. He used this fame as a springboard to something bigger. In 1950, he decided to run for the United States Senate.

SOURCE DOCUMENT

for the office who have in the past and will in the future support the Administration's socialistic program—because I am convinced that if we do not win the fight in 1950 we may never have another chance—I shall submit my name to the people of California as a candidate for United States Senator.

No Easy Battle

I am asking you tonight to join with me in the fight before us. It will not be an easy battle. It is much easier to buy votes with high-sounding promises than it is to sell a constructive and honest program.

The opposition will be well financed. A huge slush fund is even now being wrung from the hands of workers for the purpose of opposing any candidate who will not take his orders from a clique of labor lobbyists in Washington. Power hungry bureaucrats will do everything they can in behalf of the administration candidate, because they will be fighting for their own political lives.

Fighting, Rocking, Socking Campaign

There is only one way we can win. We must put on a fighting, rocking, socking campaign, and carry that campaign directly into every county, city, town, precinct and home in the State of California. I intend to wage this type of campaign, but only with the help of thousands of volunteer workers can we succeed. We will tell the people the truth. We will tell the people honestly and fearlessly where we stand on every major issue. We will raise a banner of freedom which all people can follow. If we do this, we cannot help but win.

My future, or the future of the Republican party, is not of primary importance. What is important is that this election will determine whether the people of the United States are to be dragged slowly but surely down the road toward State Socialism—or whether they will see the truth before it is too late, and take the high road which leads to freedom and the realization of the American dream.

1950 will mark the One Hundredth Anniversary of Statehood for California. The pioneers who developed the West came from all nations, all creeds, all walks of life. They found here a climate of political and economic freedom which allowed and encouraged men to produce to the maximum of their abilities. California is a great State, and America is a great nation today, because from the time of our founding we have recognized the fundamental rights and dignity of men and women as individuals—not numbers on the rolls of a Socialistic State.

Meet the Challenge

There is no better way, in the crucial year of 1950, for the people of California to express their gratitude for the blessings of freedom we enjoy in this Republic than to meet the challenge of those who are destroying that freedom. Let us lead the way by sending to the Congress and the Senate of the United States men and women who can be counted on to speak fearlessly, articulately and honestly for the principles which made our country great. On that basis, and with faith in the destiny of America, I announce my candidacy for United States Senator from California.

NIXON, the MAN--

CONGRESSMAN RICHARD NIXON was selected by the United States Junior Chamber of Commerce as one of the nation's "ten outstanding young men of 1947." A native Californian, he was born January 9, 1913, in Yorba Linda, and is a graduate of Whittier College and Duke University Law School. He practiced law in Whittier from 1937 until he joined the United States Navy in August of 1942, where he served until January, 1946, attaining the rank of lieutenant commander. Much of his service was in the South Pacific area. Congressman Nixon was married in 1940 to Patricia Ryan, and they now have two daughters, Patricia, born February, 1946, and Julie, born July, 1948. He is a member of the Friends (Quaker) Church, and is a Trustee of Whittier College.

ELECTED TO THE CONGRESS in 1946 as a Republican, over H. Jerry Voorhis, a Democratic 12th District Congressman for ten years, Congressman Nixon was reelected in 1948, receiving both the Republican and Democratic nominations at the primary election.

AS A MEMBER OF THE HOUSE COMMITTEE ON EDUCATION AND LABOR, Congressman Nixon played a leading role in drafting and supporting the Taft-Hartley Labor-Management Relations Act of 1947.

HE GAINED NATIONAL PROMINENCE by virtue of his level-headed, aggressive service on the House Committee on Un-American Activities, where he served as chairman of the Legislative Sub-Committee, and co-authored the Mundt-Nixon Communist Control Bill which passed the House by a vote of 319 to 58. He is generally credited with "breaking" the Hiss-Chambers espionage case.

CONGRESSMAN NIXON WAS A MEMBER OF THE HERTER COMMITTEE which visited Europe in the fall of 1947 to gather evidence of European needs preparatory to Congressional enactment of the European Recovery Program (Marshall Plan). This committee received much favorable recognition for its businesslike, thorough investigations and report of conditions in Europe.

CONGRESSMAN RICHARD NIXON FOR UNITED STATES SENATOR
SOUTHERN CALIFORNIA CAMPAIGN COMMITTEE
201 W. M. Garland Bldg., Los Angeles 15 · TRinity 0661
Bernard C. Brennan, Chairman · Patrick J. Hillings, Secretary

1950
The Year of Decision

CONGRESSMAN RICHARD NIXON

FOR

UNITED STATES SENATOR

This campaign brochure for the 1950 California Senate race highlights Nixon's strong points.

Again, Nixon used fear to get votes. His Democratic opponent was Congressperson Helen Gahagan Douglas. She had once been an actress on Broadway and was married to a famous movie actor named Melvyn Douglas. Nixon accused her of not strongly opposing communism. He even suggested that she sympathized with Communists.

The fear of communism was so strong that Douglas's campaign staff used the same argument against Nixon. They circulated a leaflet on yellow paper claiming Nixon was soft on communism. That strategy backfired because Nixon's anti-Communist record was solid. In the same leaflet, Douglas compared Nixon with dictators Josef Stalin and Adolf Hitler.

In response, Nixon's campaign staff distributed their own flyer to California voters. Nixon's flyer claimed that in Congress, Douglas voted 354 times to support issues viewed as pro-Communist.[11] To drive home the point, Nixon's staff had the charges printed on pink paper. It became known as the pink sheet.[12]

The feud between the two candidates continued. Douglas gave Nixon the nickname "Tricky Dick." (He would continue to be called that by political enemies throughout his career.) Then Nixon said that Douglas was "pink right down to her underwear."[13]

Nixon was not the only opponent to accuse Douglas of pro-Communist views. When she ran for the nomination of her party, some Democrats made the same charge against her.

THE NIXONS—PAT, JULIE, DICK AND TRICIA

Dear Friend:
   Every California family has a real stake in the coming election. The vote you cast, or do not cast, may determine the fate of our American way of life.
   National observers are agreed that Richard Nixon has done more constructive work to combat Communism than any other member of Congress.
   Protect your future. Vote November 7th for Congressman Richard Nixon for United States Senator.

                    Sincerely,

111

This postcard from the 1950 California Senate campaign shows Nixon with his family.

One Democrat who gave a campaign contribution to Nixon was a diplomat and wealthy businessperson. He was named Joseph Kennedy. Kennedy was a very strong anti-Communist. The contribution check was delivered by his son, Congressperson John F. Kennedy. He was the same man who had debated Nixon over the Taft-Hartley bill.

On January 21, 1950, Nixon heard the news he had been waiting for. Alger Hiss was convicted of perjury in his second trial. Hiss was then sentenced to five years in prison.

On June 24, 1950, nine thousand miles away from

The Nixon family at play.

Washington, D.C., Communists from North Korea invaded South Korea. Korea is a small country located on a peninsula bordering China. After World War II, Korea was divided into two sections. North Korea was led by a Communist government. South Korea was a democracy.

Within a week of the invasion, the United Nations voted to provide military aid to South Korea. This was the start of the Korean War. Of sixteen nations involved in the military effort, the United States provided most of the fighting forces.

The timing of the Korean War was perfect for candidate Nixon. His warnings about communism seemed to be right on target.

In November 1950, Nixon won the election for Senate by more than six hundred eighty thousand votes.[14] He was now a United States senator. Yet something even greater awaited him.

5

IKE, DICK, CHECKERS, AND JACK

At thirty-eight years old, Richard Nixon was the youngest member of the Senate.[1] Because of the Hiss case, he was better known than many who had been in the Senate for years. His appearance impressed people. No longer a skinny college kid, Nixon was just under six feet tall and weighed 175 pounds. He combed his short, wavy hair straight back.

Most of the time he wore dark, conservative suits. He had a handsome smile. However, Nixon had a heavy beard that grew in not long after shaving. Some thought it made him look sinister.

As senator, Nixon continued to warn about the dangers of communism. He also blamed President Truman for much of the trouble in the world. The

Korean War had settled into a stalemate. Neither side was winning. Nixon said the stalemate was Truman's fault for not taking stronger military action against North Korea and Communist China. He further criticized Truman for not doing more to find Communists working in the United States government.

The year 1952 was a presidential election year. Truman was not running for reelection. The Democrats selected Illinois governor Adlai Stevenson as their nominee. The Republicans chose General Dwight David Eisenhower as theirs. Eisenhower was a five-star general, the highest rank one can achieve in the Army. One of the heroes of World War II, he was an incredibly popular man.

Eisenhower had to select a running mate for the office of vice-president. It is common for presidential candidates to choose a running mate different from themselves. That way, the candidates are more likely to draw votes from a wide range of people. Since Eisenhower was sixty-two years old in 1952, a younger running mate would balance the ticket. Being a moderate Republican, Eisenhower might choose a more conservative Republican as his vice-president. Eisenhower was from Kansas, a state without a large population. It was likely he would select a running mate from a populous state.

Richard Nixon fit the bill perfectly. A conservative from California, he was only thirty-nine. It made sense that Eisenhower picked Nixon as the Republican

JOHN F. KENNEDY
11th Dist., Massachusetts

COMMITTEE:
EDUCATION AND LABOR
DISTRICT OF COLUMBIA

Congress of the United States
House of Representatives
Washington, D. C.

SECRETARY:
T. J. PEARSON, Jr.

BOSTON:
FRANCIS X. MORRISSEY
JOSEPH E. ROSETTI

A letter from Congressman John F. Kennedy congratulating Nixon on being chosen as the 1952 Republican vice-presidential candidate.

candidate for vice-president. This was only six years after Nixon entered politics.

Dick and Pat Nixon spent much time away from home campaigning. The two Nixon children had hardly known a time when their parents were not busy campaigning. When Pat told six-year-old Tricia that her daddy was running for vice-president, Tricia said in disappointment, "Oh, you mean that you're going campaigning again!"[2]

On September 18, *The New York Post*, a major newspaper, ran the following headline: "SECRET NIXON FUND."[3] A smaller headline followed: "Secret Rich Men's Trust Fund Keeps Nixon in Style Far Beyond His Salary."[4]

The article said that Nixon was given money and gifts he did not earn. It claimed these were given by wealthy Californians who expected political favors in return. It soon seemed Nixon's nomination was doomed. Some Republicans thought Nixon should withdraw from the race. Eisenhower gave Nixon a chance to respond to the charges.

On September 23, Nixon gave a talk on live television. Television was a new medium. In 1952, many Americans had just bought their first TV sets. Some had to go to neighbors' houses or restaurants to watch television. It was a novelty for a politician to give an important speech on television.

Nixon planned to speak for thirty minutes. He was nervous. Just three minutes before going on the air,

Nixon said to Pat, "I just don't think I can go through with this one."[5]

She responded, "Of course you can."[6] She then took his hand and walked with him to the stage.

Nixon gave what many today believe to be the speech of his life. He began with these words, "My fellow Americans, I come before you tonight as a candidate for the vice-presidency and as a man whose honesty and integrity have been questioned."[7]

He went on to describe in detail his personal finances. Nixon told the audience how much money his family owed on their house and on loans. Nixon wanted to assure the public that he was not rich.

Just before finishing the speech, Nixon added words that have become famous. He announced that a man in Texas had heard Pat say on the radio that Tricia and Julie would like to have a pet dog. Nixon admitted that the man had sent the Nixons one gift:

> It was a little cocker spaniel dog, in a crate, that he had sent all the way from Texas—black and white, spotted, and our little girl Tricia, the six-year-old, named it Checkers. And you know, the kids, like all kids, loved the dog, and I just want to say this, right now, that regardless of what they say about it, we are going to keep it.[8]

At first, Nixon thought the speech was a failure.[9] For one thing, it ran too long. As Nixon was still talking, an announcer broke in and said, "Time purchased for this program has now elapsed."[10]

Nixon began to think differently after a makeup

artist at the studio said there had "never been a broadcast like it."[11] Camera operators were so touched that they had tears in their eyes. The office of the Republican National Committee received three hundred thousand letters and telegrams supporting Nixon.[12] State Republican committees reported thousands more telegrams supporting Nixon by a 350 to 1 ratio.[13]

Liberal journalist Tom Wicker later said, "I think it [the speech] was a masterpiece. It's laughable now. People laugh about it. But in fact, he [Nixon] saved himself on the ticket, and I think it is not beyond consideration he may have saved the Eisenhower ticket."[14]

Not all found the speech a winner. Many Americans felt it was corny. Some still feel Nixon used this

The Nixon family enjoys the beach in Rehoboth, Delaware, in 1952.

sentimental story about a pet dog to save his career. However, the fact is that the speech did save his career. Eisenhower kept Nixon as a running mate. Nixon always referred to the speech as the "Fund speech." To nearly everyone else, including Nixon's opponents, it became known as the "Checkers speech."

Today, most historians believe the charges made by *The New York Post* and Nixon's enemies were not fair or proven. Historian Stephen Ambrose wrote, "Had they bothered to check, they would have known that whatever other sins Nixon was guilty of, they did not include high living."[15]

In November, Eisenhower and Nixon were elected president and vice-president in a landslide. They received 55.1 percent of the vote. Stevenson earned 44.4 percent. Eisenhower and Nixon got 442 electoral votes. Stevenson pulled in 89.[16]

Nixon was an active vice-president. He went on official trips to foreign countries. When President Eisenhower was away, he directed official meetings. In 1954, he made a bold announcement. In it, he publicly disagreed with the president over United States involvement in Asia. It had to do with sending American fighting men to another Asian country, Vietnam.

The Korean War ended in 1953 as a draw. Korea was left a divided country, with North Korea remaining Communist and South Korea remaining non-Communist. In spite of that, Americans were relieved that the war was over.

However, trouble was now brewing in Vietnam. When Nixon became vice-president, Vietnam was under the rule of France. In the 1950s, the Vietnamese were fighting to overthrow the French. Many in the United States were concerned that if the French were forced out, Vietnamese Communists would take over control of Vietnam.

By April 1954, it was certain that France was going to lose. At a convention of newspaper editors, Nixon was asked a serious question: Should the United States send troops to Vietnam to relieve the French if it might keep Vietnam from becoming Communist?

Nixon answered, "I believe that the executive branch of the government has to take the politically unpopular position of facing up to it and doing it, and I personally would support such a decision."[17]

With the Korean War just ended, Americans did not want to become bogged down in another war. Eisenhower disagreed with Nixon. He did not send troops to relieve the French. Like Korea, Vietnam was a country split into a north Communist division and a south non-Communist one.

Nixon came close to taking over the president's job in September 1955. Eisenhower had just suffered a heart attack and was critically ill. Nixon later wrote, "As I thought of this I realized what a tremendous responsibility had descended upon me. It was like a great physical weight holding me down in the chair."[18]

Eisenhower recovered. In 1956, he and Nixon ran

The Eisenhowers and Nixons in the White House on the eve of the 1956 presidential election.

for reelection. They defeated Adlai Stevenson again. This time the margin was even bigger than in 1952.

Eisenhower's health problems continued. In 1957, he suffered a stroke. Once again, Nixon was a heartbeat away from the presidency. And once again, Eisenhower recovered.

Nixon had his own brush with death the next year. The Nixons took an official trip to South America. They arrived at the airport in Caracas, the capital of Venezuela. Suddenly they were attacked by a mob that included local Communists. The mob threw things at the Nixons and spit in their faces and on their clothes. The vice-president and his wife were covered with a flood of brown tobacco juice.

The Nixons then rode in a motorcade through downtown Caracas. Richard Nixon was in one car, and Pat in another. Another mob surrounded the vice-president's car. The mob was made up mostly of teenagers influenced by older people. They attacked the car with pipes, beer cans, rocks, and their fists. The car's shatterproof windows were cracked in the attack. Then the mob began rocking the car, trying to overturn it.

Nixon feared for his life.[19] He later wrote, "It made me almost physically ill to see the fanatical frenzy in the eyes of teenagers—boys and girls who were little older than my twelve-year-old daughter, Tricia. My reaction was a feeling of absolute hatred for the tough Communist agitators who were driving children to this irrational state."[20]

After about ten minutes, a news truck cleared a path for the motorcade. When the Nixons returned home, they were treated as heroes.

In 1959, Nixon faced another battle. This time, it was a battle of words.

The Soviet Union and the United States agreed to hold a cultural exchange program. As part of the program, the United States held an exhibition in the Soviet capital of Moscow. The exhibition featured displays showing how Americans lived. Nixon flew to Moscow to open the exhibition on July 24, 1959.

In a reproduction of an American kitchen at the exhibition, Nixon and Soviet leader Nikita Khrushchev began an informal debate. Khrushchev spoke highly of the Communist way of life. Nixon defended capitalism. The two world leaders went toe-to-toe. A photo was taken of Nixon poking his finger into Khrushchev's chest. It ran in newspapers across the United States. Nixon looked strong. He was the hero of what became known as the "kitchen debate."

The year 1960 was a presidential election year. Nixon was the Republican nominee for president. A

Vice-President Nixon throws out the first ball on the opening day of the 1959 baseball season at Washington's Griffith Stadium.

Massachusetts senator was the Democratic nominee. It was none other than John F. Kennedy, Nixon's old friend from the House of Representatives. Jack Kennedy chose as his running mate Texas senator Lyndon Baines Johnson.

Nixon called for a strong military. He promised to continue the fight against communism. Nixon announced at the Republican convention in the summer of 1960, "When Mr. Khrushchev says our grandchildren will live under Communism, let us say his grandchildren will live in freedom."[21]

Kennedy campaigned on nearly the same issues. He, too, ran on the messages of military strength and anti-communism. Both men said they would build a better America.

It was the methods they intended to use to achieve a better America that were different. Kennedy would rely more heavily on government programs than would Nixon. Nixon had more faith in private business and smaller government.

The candidates agreed to appear on television for a series of four debates. There had never been televised presidential debates before. Yet Nixon knew he had had good luck on television in 1952 with the Checkers speech.

The first debate took place on September 26, 1960. Nixon had just spent two weeks in the hospital with a knee infection. He was pale. On the other hand, Kennedy was dark and tanned. The studio walls were light in color. Kennedy wore a dark suit and stood out against them. Nixon wore a light-colored suit and blended in with the walls. This made his complexion seem even paler. Nixon's heavy five o'clock shadow (beard stubble) did not help his appearance.

The two men stood when they spoke. Kennedy stood up straight and appeared confident. Because of his weak knee, Nixon shifted his weight when he stood. He was sweating in the warm studio and he seemed uneasy.

More than 80 million people watched the debate.[22] Millions more listened to it on the radio.

Kennedy advisor Pierre Salinger later said, "While the overwhelming number of people who saw the debates believed Kennedy had won them, the equally overwhelming number of people who only heard them, who listened on the radio, thought Nixon had won. Which shows that it is not so important what you say on television but how you present it, the fashion in which you appear on television."[23]

There were three more debates, but each drew far fewer viewers. Ultimately, in one of the closest elections in United States history, Nixon lost. Kennedy received barely one hundred thousand votes more than Nixon.[24] In a country of millions of people that is a very small amount. The electoral vote total was more decisive. Kennedy received 303 to Nixon's 219.[25]

Soon after the election, the issue of voter fraud was raised. That meant that some votes for Kennedy may have been cast illegally. If true, then Nixon really might have won the election. Votes in Chicago and Texas were questioned by Nixon supporters.

Legally, Nixon could have asked for a recount, but he did not. A recount would have taken a long time. How could the country run smoothly if there were no definite president? Nixon said a recount would have disrupted the day-to-day operations of the United States. Some historians add that Nixon had an ulterior motive for not asking for a recount. If it turned out that Kennedy really won, Nixon would look like a sore loser. That might hurt him if he ran for office later.

Nixon returned to private law practice. Politics, however, was in his blood. In 1962, he ran for governor of California. However, Nixon had not lived in California for some time and was not as familiar with state issues as his opponent, Governor Edmund (Pat) Brown. Nixon lost the election.

He was angry at the media who, he believed, had never given him a fair shake. Just after the election, Nixon spoke to the press at the Beverly Hilton Hotel in Los Angeles. He said bitterly, ". . . as I leave you I want you to know—just think how much you're going to be missing. You won't have Nixon to kick around any more, because, gentlemen, this is my last press conference. . . ."[26]

A week after the election, *Time* magazine said, ". . . barring a miracle, [Richard Nixon's] political career ended last week."[27]

6

PRESIDENT,
AT LAST

Just four months later, Nixon appeared on a television variety show called *The Jack Paar Program*. On the show, Paar presented entertainers and other famous people. It was similar to late-night programs today such as *The Late Show* with David Letterman and *The Tonight Show* with Jay Leno.

The date was March 8, 1963. It was Nixon's first public appearance since he lost the race for governor of California.[1] He had moved to New York City, where he was working as a lawyer for a private law firm. On Paar's show, Nixon was relaxed and in good spirits. He played on the piano a catchy little song he had written.

Then, he sat with Paar, and they joked around while discussing news events of the day. Paar asked Nixon if he was once friends with President Kennedy. Nixon answered yes. He continued, "We came to Congress together and we were low men on the totem pole, on the Labor Committee together. And we remained low men until he ran for president. Now he's up and I'm down."[2] Nixon, Paar, and the audience all laughed loudly. Nobody could have imagined what would happen eight months later.

On November 22, 1963, President Kennedy was assassinated in Dallas, Texas. Vice-President Lyndon Johnson became president. Less than a year later, Johnson won easily when he ran for president in his own right.

Nixon spent the next few years campaigning for Republican candidates and traveling throughout the world. In doing so, he kept his name in the public eye. Politics was still his main interest, and the presidency was always on his mind.

At the same time, major changes were taking place overseas in Vietnam. Although President Eisenhower had not sent any combat troops to Vietnam, he did send military advisors. Their job was to instruct the South Vietnamese on ways to fight the Communists. President Kennedy also sent military advisors to South Vietnam.

In 1965, Lyndon Johnson became the first president to send combat troops to Vietnam. Over the next few years, he sent more and more troops. By 1968, more than five hundred thousand American troops were fighting in Vietnam.[3] Most of the men had been drafted for military service.

As American involvement in Vietnam increased, the war began to divide the country bitterly. Some Americans believed the United States had a moral duty to fight communism anywhere in the world. They argued that if Vietnam fell to Communist rule, other countries in the region would follow. It was thought these countries would then topple like dominoes. This reasoning became known as the domino theory.

Others doubted the domino theory. They believed the Vietnamese were fighting a civil war, just as the Americans had done a hundred years earlier. They also felt that the government of South Vietnam, which the United States supported, was corrupt even if it was not Communist. Why should the United States support a corrupt government, they wondered.

Many on both sides believed the United States was fighting a war it could not win. That led to further debate. Should the United States withdraw all its troops right away? Or should they withdraw gradually and give South Vietnam a chance to build up its military? Then again, some did not wish to quit at all until the Communists were defeated.

Meanwhile, hundreds of young American men were dying every week in battle. At home, thousands resisted the draft. Some found legal ways to avoid military service. Others moved to Canada. Still others burned their draft cards in public. They were arrested and jailed for doing so.

College students across the nation protested against

the war in huge numbers. They demonstrated in the streets and on campuses. People supporting the war took part in their own protest demonstrations against the antiwar college students.

Each group's opinions soon stretched beyond the war itself. To many protesting the war, those supporting the war were ignorant bigots who believed the United States should force its ways upon other countries. To many supporting the war, the antiwar protesters were spoiled, unpatriotic cowards who did not know how good they had things.

Historian Stephen Ambrose later said, "Except for the [U.S.] Civil War, the American people have never been so badly divided as they were then."[4]

Early in 1968, Lyndon Johnson announced he would not run for another term as president. The war had became too much for him. This might be the very miracle *Time* magazine had referred to in 1962. The United States was hungry for a strong leader.

Nixon earned the Republican nomination. Then he campaigned for the presidency. A major part of Nixon's campaign was his claim that he had a secret plan to end the war. His running mate was Governor Spiro Agnew of Maryland.

The Democratic candidate was Johnson's vice-president, Hubert Humphrey. That year, there was also a strong third-party candidate. He was George Wallace, former governor of Alabama. Wallace was a conservative Democrat who appealed to persons who supported the war and were fed up with the student protests. Nixon did, too. However, his supporters tended not to be as extreme as Wallace's.

Nixon won a very close election. His margin over Humphrey was less than one percent. He won with only 43.4 percent of the vote.[5] (The electoral vote total was more decisive. Nixon received 301 to Humphrey's 191. Wallace received 46.)[6]

It was a happy time for the president-elect. On December 22, his daughter Julie was married. The groom was Dwight David Eisenhower II, known as David. He was the grandson of Nixon's former boss, President Eisenhower. David and Julie had played together as children. Whoever knew they would marry each other more than ten years later?

On January 20, 1969, Nixon was sworn in as the thirty-seventh president of the United States. In the same month, Vietnam War peace talks began in Paris. Those taking part were the United States, North Vietnam, South Vietnam, and the Viet Cong (South Vietnamese rebels who supported communism).

After five months of peace talks, there was still no progress. On June 4, Nixon announced that he would gradually begin to withdraw American troops. A total of twenty-five thousand combat troops were to be back home by the end of August.[7] The plan was for some American servicemen to remain behind to help the Vietnamese more strongly defend their country. When that was accomplished, Americans would withdraw in

RICHARD M. NIXON

November 22, 1967

Dear Julie -
I suppose no father believes
any boy is good enough for
his daughter.
But I believe both
David and you are lucky
to have found each other —
Fina often says — "Miss Julie
always brings life into the home."
In the many years ahead
you will have ups and downs
but I know you will always
"bring life into your home" wherever
it is — love
Daddy

In this letter written to his daughter Julie just before her marriage, Nixon gives her and fiancé David Eisenhower his blessings.

greater numbers. Nixon called this the "Vietnamization" of the war.

To those who opposed the war, this gradual solution was not fast enough. A large number of Americans wanted immediate withdrawal. On October 15, they held a special Vietnam Moratorium day. Across the country, government leaders and others spoke at rallies and condemned the ongoing fighting in Vietnam.

Nixon publicly ignored the protests. He was busy making plans for a speech. With hundreds of thousands of Americans protesting the war, Nixon wanted to assure the public that he was doing all he could to end the war honorably. If the Checkers speech was the

Nixon meets with troops in Vietnam in 1969.

speech of Nixon's life, this would have to be the speech of his presidency.

On the evening of November 3, 1969, Nixon appeared on television. After explaining his goal of a gradual withdrawal of troops, he said he would now speak directly to the many young protesters.

Nixon said, "I respect your idealism. I share your concern for peace. I want peace as much as you do. . . . I want to end the war to save the lives of those brave young men in Vietnam. I want to end it in a way which will increase the chance that their younger brothers and their sons will not have to fight in some future Vietnam some place in the world."[8]

Nixon then referred to a protest sign he had seen. The message on the sign urged the United States to lose the war and call all the troops home right away. Nixon said that most Americans do not share that viewpoint.

"If a vocal minority, however fervent its cause, prevails over reason and the will of the majority, this nation has no future as a free society. So tonight, to you, the great silent majority of my fellow Americans, I ask for your support."[9]

As with the Checkers speech eighteen years earlier, the response was overwhelming. More than eighty thousand letters and telegrams were sent by American citizens to the White House. Nearly all supported Nixon.[10] The talk later became known as the "Silent Majority" speech.

To many historians, the Silent Majority speech

Nixon in the Oval Office with Secretary of State William Rogers (left) and National Security Advisor Henry Kissinger on March 6, 1969.

represented the heart and soul of Richard Nixon. The "silent majority" were the people who came from the same background as Nixon. They were patriotic, working-class people, just as Nixon's family was. To Nixon, the college protesters were like the Franklins back at Whittier College—pampered and privileged. The silent majority were like Nixon's own Orthogonians—patriotic and practical.

Yet the protests did not stop. On November 15, a March Against Death took place in Washington, D.C. More than three hundred thousand people came to the nation's capital to protest against American involvement in the war.[11]

Over the long, cold winter, college campuses were fairly quiet. That ended on April 30, 1970.

The country of Cambodia borders Vietnam. In 1970, it was a neutral country. That means it did not take sides in the fighting. However, both South Vietnam and the Viet Cong used Cambodia as an unofficial battleground. Some Viet Cong made bases in Cambodia and used them to attack the South Vietnamese. Then they could return to the safety of "neutral" Cambodia.

In March 1970, an anti-Communist general named Lon Nol overthrew the neutral government in Cambodia. Soon Lon Nol's government was attacked by North Vietnamese Communists.

On April 30, Nixon publicly announced he was sending American troops into Cambodia to fight what he saw as a serious threat to the anti-Communist government. The troops were to clean out the Communists. Nixon promised that the American fighting forces would be out by June 30. He said the invasion of Cambodia was necessary to end the war quickly.

To those against the war, just the opposite seemed true. To them, Nixon was expanding the war by invading still another nation. College campuses awoke from their relative quiet and exploded in protest. Not all acts of protest were nonviolent. Some blew up into riots. On some campuses, students tried to destroy buildings housing Reserve Officers Training Corps (ROTC) offices. The ROTC is part of the United States military services.

On May 1, a reporter overheard Nixon speaking to a

woman whose husband was a soldier in Vietnam. Nixon said to her, "You see these bums . . . blowing up the campuses. Listen, the boys that are on the college campuses today are the luckiest people in the world, going to the greatest universities, and here they are burning up the books, storming around about this issue."[12]

The comment made headlines across the country. Nixon then insisted the only students he called "bums" were the ones who resorted to violence.[13] But some Americans had the impression that Nixon was calling all protesters bums.

One of the many campuses where protests were taking place was Kent State University in Ohio. In order to break up the protests, Ohio governor James Rhodes called in the National Guard to restore order.

Students taunted the National Guard. A few threw rocks. Suddenly, some of the Guard fired their guns at the students. Four students were killed and nine were wounded.[14] Some were protesters. Others were innocent bystanders.

The father of one girl who was killed said to the press, "My child was not a bum."[15] It was a direct response to Nixon.

Nixon's daughter Julie later wrote about the incident, "My father would admit later that those few days after Kent State were among the darkest of his Presidency. What made the period so bleak was the . . . gulf between those who opposed the war for what they believed were all the right reasons and the president who wanted to end it 'honorably' for what he believed were all the right reasons."[16]

Again, masses of protesters came to Washington. A National Day of Protest was scheduled for May 9. Nixon was deeply troubled.[17] At about 4 A.M. on May 9, Nixon told Secret Service agents he wanted to talk with the protesters. They arranged for a car to drive Nixon to the middle of the protest. For a half hour, Nixon and the protesters talked.

One student told Nixon, "I hope you realize we are willing to die for what we believe in." Nixon responded, "Many of us when we were your age were also willing to die for what we believed in." The president added, "We are trying to build a world in which you will not have to die for what you believe in."[18] As dawn began to break, the Secret Service became concerned for Nixon's safety. He was rushed back to the White House.

Protests continued as Nixon's effort at the Vietnamization of the war was continuing. More troops were brought home. There were five hundred forty-three thousand American men fighting in Vietnam in 1969. By the end of 1970, that number was reduced to three hundred forty thousand.[19] As Nixon promised, United States fighting forces were withdrawn from Cambodia two months later. However, Secretary of State William Rogers said later that, as it turned out, the entrance into Cambodia contributed nothing to end the war more quickly.[20]

At home, other issues were facing Americans. The nation's cities were choking with air pollution. Its rivers and lakes were being used by industries as garbage dumps. Today most Americans are aware of the need for clean air and water. However, throughout the 1950s and much of the 1960s, little attention was paid to this problem.

In the late 1960s some groups concerned with the quality of the air and water began to protest publicly. On April 22, 1970, the antipollution protest movement reached a peak. The day was declared Earth Day. Millions across the country attended rallies and programs celebrating the importance of a clean environment. Unlike the Vietnam War protests, these were peaceful.

Nixon said he agreed with the cause. He stated, "Clean air, clean water, open spaces—these should once again be the birthright of every American."[21] In 1970, Nixon established a government agency called the Environmental Protection Agency (EPA). A major role of the EPA is to monitor the quality of air and water.

This was a fairly liberal idea for a conservative Republican. In fact, Nixon was responsible for other programs in which government plays an active role. For example, his administration established the Occupational Safety and Health Administration (OSHA). OSHA helps maintain safe conditions for workers. Some business owners object to OSHA. They say it makes unnecessary demands on them and they believe it costs too much time and money to meet OSHA requirements.

In 1971, Nixon took another unusual step for a conservative. Prices of items from food to cars were rapidly increasing. To slow this trend, Nixon introduced wage and price controls. Business owners were not allowed to raise either prices or workers' salaries. It was a clear case of the government regulating how business owners can run their companies.

Why did Nixon make so many policies that could be considered more Democratic than Republican? Nixon's chief economic advisor, Herb Stein, said that the unemployment rate was at about 6 percent.[22] At the time, that was considered high. The media and leading members of Congress urged Nixon to use his power as president to do something.

Stein added, "I think you shouldn't label Nixon as a fiscal conservative. [The word *fiscal* refers to a government's taxing and spending policies.] He liked to think of himself as open-minded to new ideas. He regarded himself as a free-thinking statesman, as he was in many respects. I describe him as a conservative man with liberal ideas."[23]

A happy event took place in the White House on June 12, 1971. Tricia Nixon married an attorney named Edward Cox in a lavish White House wedding. However, every bit of good news seemed to take a backseat to the Vietnam War.

A new development was occurring. On June 13,

1971, the *New York Times,* one of the most important newspapers in the United States, published the first portion of what became known as the Pentagon Papers. These papers were secret documents from the U.S. Department of Defense. (The Pentagon is the name of the building just outside Washington, D.C., where the Department of Defense has its headquarters.) The documents discussed the United States involvement in Vietnam over the previous years.

The documents were given to the *Times* by a Defense Department researcher named Daniel Ellsberg. He did not give them to the *Times* in a legal way. On the contrary, he gave them secretly. This is called leaking.

Ellsberg had once supported the war. By 1971 he had changed his views. He said he leaked the documents, "to impress on the people that every other president had lied [about Vietnam] and that he [Nixon] might too."[24]

At first Nixon was not concerned about the Pentagon Papers.[25] They were about earlier presidents. However, one of Nixon's staff members was extremely concerned. He was National Security Advisor Henry Kissinger. Kissinger believed other countries would lose faith in the United States government if it seemed it could not control its own secret documents.[26]

Within a month, Nixon told a staff member named Egil (Bud) Krogh to put together a secret team to stop such leaks. This group assigned to stop leaks was called "the plumbers."

SOURCE DOCUMENT

June 12, 1971
12:10 AM

THE WHITE HOUSE
WASHINGTON

Dear Tricia –

Well Today is the day you begin a long and exciting journey –

I want you to know how proud I have been of you through the years – some of them – pretty difficult for you I'm sure.

The years ahead will be happy ones because you will make them so.

Your strength of character will see you through whatever comes – You have made the right choice and I am sure Eddie + you will look back on this time and be able to say –

"The day indeed was splendid."

Love —
Daddy

A letter of encouragement from Nixon to his daughter Tricia on her wedding day. Notice how he signs the letter "Daddy." Tricia was married to Edward Cox, an attorney, on June 12, 1971.

Two members of the plumbers team went one step farther. In September, E. Howard Hunt and G. Gordon Liddy broke into the office of a psychiatrist Ellsberg was seeing. They tried to find information that would make Ellsberg look bad. They found none. However, by breaking into a private office, they had broken the law.

The public knew nothing about this break-in at the time it happened. The big news was Nixon's history-making trip to China in February 1972. Just three months later, Nixon made another historic journey. He went to the Soviet Union to sign a treaty with the country he had once feared and hated.

It was the first official visit of a United States president to the Soviet Union.[27] Nixon and Soviet Union premier Leonid Brezhnev signed an agreement to limit the strategic weapons of each country. The agreement became known as the Strategic Arms Limitation Talks (SALT).

Did Nixon's China trip have something to do with the USSR's signing a peace treaty so quickly? Was the Nixon staff correct to predict that making friends with the USSR's enemy would cause the USSR to become more friendly? It certainly seemed so.

Less than a month later, on June 17, 1972, an unrelated incident took place. Five men were arrested for breaking into the headquarters of the Democratic National Committee in Virginia, just outside Washington, D.C. The offices were located in the Watergate apartment and office complex. Few, if any, knew at the time that this burglary would be the beginning of the end for Nixon's presidency.

7

THE NATIONAL
NIGHTMARE

In reporting the Watergate break-in, television newscaster Sam Donaldson said the following:

> The Democratic National Committee is trying to solve a spy mystery. It began before dawn Saturday when five intruders were captured by police inside the offices of the committee in Washington. The five men carried cameras and apparently had planted electronic bugs. One of them had several crisp, new one hundred dollar bills in his pocket. The Democrats say they have no idea who would want to spy on them.[1]

The five men were members of the Committee to Reelect the President (CRP). (The committee became known to Nixon's enemies as CREEP.) Nobody imagined that the president had anything to do with this burglary.

The biggest story on people's minds during the

summer of 1972 was the upcoming presidential election. The Democrats nominated South Dakota senator George McGovern to run against Nixon.

Many Americans saw McGovern as too liberal for the good of the country. They felt Nixon had a more moderate and rational plan to end the war. However, McGovern was no coward in the face of battle. He had been a fighter pilot in World War II. McGovern had even earned the Distinguished Flying Cross award. Yet he thought the Vietnam War was a grave mistake. He believed the United States should get out as soon as possible.

George Wallace, the governor of Alabama, who had run on a third party ticket in 1968, was out of the race. He had been shot by a would-be assassin named Arthur Bremer in May and was left paralyzed. He was in no condition to run for president.

With McGovern appearing too liberal and Wallace out of the race, Nixon seemed to be in great shape for the presidential election. In addition, the country appeared to be on the right track.

Nixon's successful trips to China and the Soviet Union had just taken place. The United States presence in Vietnam was winding down. By 1972, there were only twenty-five thousand United States troops remaining in Vietnam.[2] Most were not fighting men but military advisors. Wage and price controls were loosened.

That same year Nixon's pen continued to be busy as he signed various bills into law. One was at the time a little regarded measure known as Title IX of the Education Amendments of 1972. It prohibits gender discrimination in any educational program receiving federal funding. Included are sports activities, which means that girls' and women's school sports teams could thrive as men's had for years. Since few people suspected Nixon had anything to do with the Watergate burglary, that was not a major issue.[3]

In November, Nixon won the largest victory of any president in the history of the electoral college until that time. He captured forty-nine of the fifty states. McGovern carried only Massachusetts. Nixon earned 60.7 percent of the vote; McGovern received only 37.5 percent.[4]

Just after the start of 1973, the peace talks in Paris reached a conclusion. On January 27, Henry Kissinger, who was by then secretary of state, and North Vietnam representative Le Duc Tho signed a peace treaty. The United States would withdraw its remaining military forces. Some civilian advisors would stay. North Vietnam would release all United States prisoners of war. A cease-fire was declared.

To many, Nixon was a hero for finally ending the fighting. Others shared the opinion of George McGovern. He said Nixon withdrew the troops four years too late. McGovern believed that "he [Nixon] could have negotiated a settlement his first year in office. The terms we got in 1973 were no better than the ones we could have had in 1969."[5]

The cost of the war in terms of human life was horrible. A total of fifty-eight thousand Americans died in the conflict. Another three hundred four thousand were wounded.[6] Although the United States was now out of the struggle, North and South Vietnam continued to fight each other.

At home, Nixon had his own battles. The Watergate burglars were facing trial. Two more men were named in the crime. They were G. Gordon Liddy and E. Howard Hunt. Liddy and Hunt were accused of directing the burglary.

Hunt and four other men pleaded guilty to conspiracy and burglary. Liddy and one CRP burglar, James McCord, pleaded not guilty but were eventually found guilty. Then on February 7, the United States Senate voted to set up a special committee. The committee had the assignment of trying to discover if any other laws were broken during the Nixon campaign of 1972.

The committee received a boost on March 20. James McCord gave a private letter to the judge who was over-seeing the trial, John J. Sirica. In it, McCord made many statements that were damaging to the Nixon administration. McCord's greatest charge was that powerful men in the White House had pressured the Watergate burglars not to tell the truth. Another was that the defendants committed perjury by lying during the trial.

Political scientists and others guessed that McCord

wrote the letter because he did not want to be punished while guilty people in higher positions went free.[7]

McCord was called to testify before the special Senate committee. Other important people who worked for Nixon were soon accused of wrongdoing. One was Jeb Stuart Magruder, the deputy director of the CRP. Another was John Dean, a leading advisor to the president. Two more were John Ehrlichman and H. R. (Bob) Haldeman. They were also advisors to Nixon.

The whole affair began to unravel on television before the nation's eyes in the summer of 1973. To find the truth, the Senate Watergate Committee held hearings. These were televised daily. Members of the committee asked questions of people who worked with Nixon. Those answering questions, or testifying, had to swear to tell all the truth, just as if they were in a court of law.

On June 25, John Dean told the committee that President Nixon was involved in a cover-up of the investigation into the Watergate burglary. That meant that Nixon was trying to stop investigators from getting honest answers. Dean also revealed that the Nixon staff had an "enemies list." These were names of people thought to be unfriendly to Nixon. It included famous politicians, entertainers, and journalists. Dean admitted that he and an advisor to Nixon named Charles Colson had prepared the list.

People on the enemies list would possibly be harassed. Some would be banned from special White

House functions. Others would be followed by private detectives.

Dean's information was very damaging to Nixon. But one question remained: Was Dean telling the truth?

Less than a month later, there was another confession. The date was Friday, July 13. It proved to be unlucky for the president. Alexander Butterfield was another aide to Nixon. Butterfield told the committee a startling fact. He said Nixon had taped all private conversations that took place in his office since 1970. Nixon was planning to use the tapes someday, once he was out of office, to write his memoirs. Now, if the committee listened to the tapes, they could perhaps find out the truth.

The problem was that the tapes belonged to Nixon. Archibald Cox held the position of independent prosecutor. One of Cox's jobs was to obtain evidence related to the case. Cox issued a written order called a subpoena. The subpoena said that Nixon must turn over several tapes to the Senate committee.

Nixon refused to do so. He insisted that as president he had "executive privilege," meaning he had special rights that an average citizen might not have. For example, if something said to the president might affect national security, the president should have a right to keep the matter private.

A legal struggle between Nixon and Cox took place well into the autumn. While this was going on, there was another bombshell. Vice-President Agnew suddenly resigned from office on October 10. Agnew was involved in a scandal unrelated to Watergate. He was charged with taking bribes and not paying his income taxes honestly.

On the same day he resigned, Agnew pleaded nolo contendere. That meant he was not contesting the charges. It was very close to pleading guilty. However, it left Agnew open to deny the charges in the future. Agnew was fined ten thousand dollars and placed on probation for three years.[8]

By now, many Americans were convinced that the entire Nixon administration was dishonest. To replace Agnew, Nixon selected Michigan congressperson Gerald Ford. The nomination of Ford as vice-president was quickly approved by Congress.

Just two days later, a court of law ordered Nixon to turn over the tapes to the Senate committee. Nixon still refused to do so. A week later, he ordered Cox to be fired. By doing so, Nixon appeared to be interfering with an official investigation. He seemed to be saying that he was above the law. The news stunned the nation.

On the night of October 20, 1973, NBC news anchor John Chancellor said on television, "Good evening. The country tonight is in the midst of what may be the most serious constitutional crisis in its history."[9]

Even many of those who had supported Nixon thought he had gone too far this time. Nixon's critics began to refer to the incident as the "Saturday Night

Massacre." As had happened before, Americans sent thousands of telegrams to the White House. This time most opposed Nixon.

Protesters demanded that he be impeached. Impeachment involves forcing the president to face hearings in the House of Representatives. Those running the hearings would decide whether or not he was guilty of certain crimes. If guilty, he would be removed from the office of president.

Within a week, a special House of Representatives committee called the Judiciary Committee introduced twenty-one bills of impeachment.[10] Nixon then released some of his tapes. It was discovered that eighteen and a half minutes were missing on one tape. Electronics experts said the tape was not faulty. That large segment of the tape had been erased by a person. Was it an accident or was it done on purpose? By this time, people were assuming the worst.

The tapes were humiliating to Nixon. He was heard swearing. That did not seem very presidential. Yet the tapes still did not provide evidence proving Nixon was involved in any crimes.

On April 11, 1974, the House Judiciary Committee subpoenaed forty-two more tapes. On April 29, Nixon announced he would release edited copies of the tapes. The committee was not satisfied. They continued to request the actual unedited tapes. Nixon still said no.

In June, the president played the role of statesman once more. He took an official trip to both the Middle

East and the Soviet Union. However, the trip was overshadowed by his problems at home. On July 24, the United States Supreme Court ruled that Nixon would have to turn over the remaining tapes. An assistant to Archibald Cox named Henry Ruth later said, "For the first time, you really had a ruling that a president of the United States is not above the law."[11]

Following the court's ruling, Nixon turned over the tapes. In late July, the House Judiciary Committee recommended impeachment of President Nixon. The vote was 27–11.[12]

An impeachment trial would likely have lasted at least half a year. Nixon said that would have given the United States a "crippled, half-time President."[13] Nixon noted he did not want the country to suffer that way. There was only one other choice. He would quit.

Nixon later said, "Resigning was the option I just didn't want to do, above everything else personally. I'm a fighter. I just didn't want to quit. Also, I thought it would be an admission of guilt—which of course it was. And also I felt that it would set a terribly bad precedent for the future. I hope no other president ever resigns under any circumstances."[14]

Nixon told his family on August 2, 1974. He later said that after telling the news to daughter Tricia, "She got up, she came over to me, put her arms around me, kissed me on the forehead, tears coming into her eyes and she said, 'You're the most decent man I've ever known.' And I said, 'Well, I just hope I haven't let you down.' But I know I had."[15]

On August 5, the contents of one of the tapes were made public. It was the tape that had been made on June 23, 1972, just nine days after the Watergate burglary. On the tape Nixon is talking with his chief of staff, H. R. Haldeman. Haldeman appears to suggest to Nixon that the CIA could be used to stop the FBI from investigating the burglary. Nixon agrees. To many, this was proof that Nixon had ordered a cover-up. This tape became forever known as the smoking gun tape. A gun that has just been fired still has smoke coming from it minutes later. This is strong evidence in a murder case, just as that tape appeared to be strong evidence against Nixon.

Nixon always denied that he planned to cover up any investigation. He later explained that his comments on the smoking gun tape took place at the end of a long day. He later added:

> I made a very stupid mistake. I said, 'Fine. Go ahead and do it.' As far as my motive was concerned . . . you just don't look at the words said at a time. You look at it in terms of what you did and what you did later. . . . Just two weeks later Pat Gray [Director of the FBI] called me on the phone. He said he was concerned about this contacting the CIA. . . . I said, 'Go right ahead with your investigation.' I didn't stop there. I called up Haldeman and Ehrlichman and said we cannot have a cover-up.[16]

Others do not agree. When asked if Nixon was directly involved in the original break-in or the cover-up, aide Herb Stein said the following: "I don't think he had any inkling of the break-in. I think he was involved in the cover-up. That's what was finally revealed by the tapes and the smoking gun and his attempt to use the CIA to cover the story up."[17]

On the evening of August 8, Nixon went on national television. He announced to the nation that he was resigning the presidency as of noon the next day. The next morning, Nixon gathered with his family in the East Room of the White House. He said a few last words to the media and the nation. At that time he gave some good advice to those listening: "Always give your best. Never get discouraged. Never be petty. Always remember others may hate you. But those who hate you

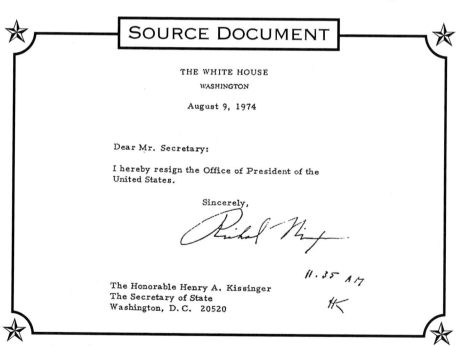

Nixon's letter of resignation to Secretary of State Henry Kissinger. Nixon was the only president ever to resign from office.

don't win unless you hate them. And then you destroy yourself."[18]

Do you think Nixon followed his own advice?

Herb Stein, who was there, recalled the moment:

> The whole staff was assembled there and we were all crying. This was a man for whom we had real affections, who had been very good to many of us, and who we thought had lots of abilities and who was being brought down by a terrible sequence of events, some mistakes, some opposition. And so we were sorry for him to have achieved what he had achieved and have overcome many obstacles and to have it collapse like that. So it was very sad.[19]

Nixon's former opponent George McGovern noted, "It's a tragedy because he had a great opportunity in that second term, I think, to move the world in a more peaceful direction."[20]

At noon on August 9, 1974, Gerald Ford was sworn in as the thirty-eighth president of the United States.

8

THE FALL
AND RISE OF
RICHARD NIXON

It would have been difficult in the second half of 1974 to find anyone as depressed as Richard Nixon. He was the first United States president to resign his office and he did so in disgrace. He was about to be tried for alleged crimes relating to Watergate, ranging from obstruction of justice to perjury, or lying under oath. He was a despised man in America and he knew it. Television show hosts made constant jokes at his expense and a slew of anti-Nixon books were published.

Liberals and others who had hated Nixon were thrilled to see him go. However, even conservative Republicans were now blasting him. While some continued to stand by Nixon, many saw him as the man who shamed their party. Nixon later wrote that he understood the criticism from those who had never liked him. However, he said that the disapproving remarks from those who had been friends were "a bit hard to take."[1]

Another president, Harry Truman, once said, "If you want a friend in Washington, buy a dog."[2] Nixon knew just what Truman had meant.

The former president and first lady moved permanently into their home in San Clemente, California, and rarely went out in public. Americans were ready to carry on under their new president. A large number wanted justice taken against Nixon. Then on September 8, exactly one month after Nixon resigned, a bombshell was dropped.

President Ford appeared on national television that morning and with no prior warning, announced he was granting Nixon a "full, free and absolute pardon" for any crimes he "has committed or may have committed or taken part in during the period from January 20, 1969, through August 9, 1974."[3]

That meant Nixon would not go to trial, nor would he be punished for any Watergate-related crimes. Nixon later wrote, "Next to the resignation, accepting the pardon was the most painful decision of my political career."[4]

Ford felt that by pardoning Nixon the country could move forward instead of dwelling on the scandal. He felt Nixon was not escaping punishment for his wrongdoings, since resigning the presidency was punishment itself. He also wondered whether Nixon could ever get a fair trial. But he also knew his decision to pardon Nixon would not be popular among a large number of Americans.

Ford was right in that regard. Reaction was strongly negative. Ford's approval rating dropped like a thermometer in January, going from seventy-one percent to forty-nine percent.[5] Even so, Ford was surprised at how intense the reaction was.

Looking back years later, Ford wrote,

> What I had failed to anticipate was the vehemence of the hostile reaction to my decision. Some of Nixon's critics apparently wanted to see him drawn and quartered publicly. They wanted a body, some broken bones or at least some blood on the floor, and their mood was mean. I thought people would consider his resignation from the Presidency as sufficient punishment and shame. I thought there would be greater forgiveness. It was one of the greatest disappointments of my presidency that everyone focused on the individual instead of on the problems the nation faced.[6]

Nixon knew enough to keep a low profile. He became a virtual recluse in his San Clemente home in a kind of self-imposed exile.

Then things got even worse. One night in September, Nixon woke in the middle of the night with a stabbing pain in his lower left abdomen. A doctor examined Nixon and diagnosed him with phlebitis, or the swelling of the blood vessels, in his left leg. Nixon's case was so extreme that his leg had swelled to three times its normal size and the condition threatened his life. The former president spent the next several days at home, his left leg in a raised position, to help reduce the swelling, and his mind filled with depressing thoughts. There were reports in the media that he seriously considered committing suicide, although his friends and family denied those as ridiculous rumors.

Nixon's acquaintances, including friends and co-workers such as Secretary of State Henry Kissinger and 1964 Republican presidential nominee Barry Goldwater, tried to raise his spirits by visiting him in San Clemente. On January 9, 1975, Pat stunned her husband with a surprise birthday party attended by friends and family. Nixon proposed a toast to all who were gathered: "Never dwell on the past. Always look to the future."[7]

Though underweight and melancholy, Nixon was slowly recovering. On February 9, he left San Clemente for the first time in three months. He drove a couple of hours to the town of Rancho Mirage in the California desert for a week-long visit with his friend, publisher Walter Annenberg. Gradually he emerged from his San Clemente cocoon more and more often and on February 21, 1976, made a trip overseas. Nixon and Pat flew to China, a place he was still respected. It was Nixon's first visit there since his historic 1972 trip.

But like many of Nixon's actions, his China trip was not without controversy. Many people, even conservative Republicans such as columnist William F. Buckley, blasted Nixon for making such a trip, saying he was doing something only the sitting president should do.

Ford, to his credit, announced that as a private citizen Nixon was entitled to go wherever he wished.

Nixon met formally with Chinese leaders and was well received. In the south China city of Canton, the Nixons were cheered by tens of thousands of jubilant Chinese citizens. Nixon flew home on February 29 knowing that in spite of the objections of many Americans, the trip was a smashing success. Secretary of State Henry Kissinger asked for a detailed account of Nixon's meetings with China's leaders, and Nixon was happy to offer one. Numerous historians say this was his first step on the long journey to respectability once more.

A presidential election was held on November 2. Sitting President Gerald Ford lost a very close vote to Democrat Jimmy Carter. Ford's pardon of Nixon definitely hurt him. In exit polls taken of voters on election day, a total of seven percent of Carter voters said the pardon was the reason they voted for the Democrat.[8] If Ford had received that seven percent, he would have beaten Carter with ease.

Nixon, meanwhile, was busy in San Clemente working on his autobiography. Then in March and April 1977 he sat down with respected British journalist David Frost for twelve days of interviews, his first since he resigned the presidency.

Sharply edited portions of the interviews aired in May. The first was televised on May 4, 1977, and it received the largest audience in history for a news interview.[9]

Frost asked hard-hitting questions and Nixon gave surprisingly open answers. For example, Nixon said of his last days in office that he had many difficult meetings including one where he broke into tears. He admitted, "It was the first time I cried since Eisenhower died."[10] At one point during the interviews, Nixon confessed, "I'm not a very lovable man."[11]

However, what became his most famous quote from the interview series referred to setting his enemies up to destroy him. Nixon admitted, "I brought myself down. I gave them a sword. And they stuck it in."[12]

As usual, liberals saw in the interviews everything they disliked about Nixon. And conservatives found in them everything they admired about him. To Nixon's financial benefit, he was paid five hundred forty thousand dollars for the interviews.[13] He greatly needed the money to pay massive legal expenses stemming from Watergate.

The interview telecasts also put Nixon back in the public eye. Then in 1978 his autobiography was published. It became a top seller. Later that year Nixon made a trip to Oxford University in England, his second trip overseas since leaving the White House. He gave speeches and answered students' questions. While some Oxford students protested his visit, his stay was generally a pleasant one.

Nixon was out of his shell, and was by now living a

life similar to that of any other ex-president. He spent his time writing books, answering mail, taking a daily afternoon swim, and going on two-mile walks. He had always been a baseball fan and on occasion drove to nearby Anaheim to attend an Angels game where he would sit in a private area near the press box.

Another step towards his comeback came in January 1979 when President Jimmy Carter invited him to the White House. Carter had just announced an official return to normal relations with China. On January 29, Nixon, Carter, and China's leaders enjoyed a former dinner in the White House. It was Nixon's first time in the president's home since August 8, 1974.

But Nixon missed his children and grandchildren. There he was in California while Julie, her husband, and daughter lived outside Philadelphia. Tricia, her husband, and young son resided in New York City. Since Nixon still needed money for legal bills, he sold the San Clemente estate in 1980 and moved to New York City where he would be closer to his family. The next year the Nixons said goodbye to city life and relocated to nearby Saddle River, New Jersey, where they lived in a handsome home in the well-to-do suburb.

However, his rise to respectability was hardly complete. The Republican party held their 1984 convention in Dallas. It is common for past presidents to speak at their parties' conventions. Republican Ronald Reagan was the sitting president and at the time was enormously popular. He was practically assured of a landslide victory in the November election. However, Nixon was not invited to speak, or even to attend the convention. Too many Americans still linked his name with Watergate.

Nixon did not let that slight stop him. In April 1986 he was asked to speak at a convention of the American Newspaper Publishers Association. The publishers loved his talk about world affairs and acknowledged that with a standing ovation. During a question and answer session afterwards, one audience member asked Nixon what he learned from Watergate. Nixon cracked, "Just destroy all the tapes."[14]

A month later Nixon's smiling face appeared on the cover of a major magazine, *Newsweek*, with the headline, "HE'S BACK: THE REHABILITATION OF RICHARD NIXON." It was a very admirable portrayal of the former president. One of President Reagan's staff members was quoted as saying, "As far as this White House is concerned, his rehabilitation is complete. There's tremendous respect for him around here."[15]

Late in 1989, as people all over the world were anticipating the start of a new decade, some startling news in Europe made one of Nixon's predictions come true. In 1960, Nixon famously professed to Soviet Union Premier Nikita Khrushchev that his grandchildren would live in freedom. Having had enough of life under communism, the residents of the Soviet Union and its eastern European satellites rebelled in the streets against communist leadership. One European

The dedication day of the Richard Nixon Library and Birthplace, July 9, 1990. Present were (from left to right) Presidents Ronald Reagan, Richard Nixon, George H.W. Bush, and Gerald Ford.

communist government after another fell, giving way to democratic leadership. The biggest was the Soviet Union. It would no longer exist as one country as all its republics became independent nations, including its biggest: Russia.

Every United States president since Herbert Hoover, the nation's thirty-first, has had a presidential library built. Unlike city and school libraries, these complexes hold each president's official papers and other artifacts. A portion of each library is set up as a museum for tourists and school groups to visit. Presidential libraries are usually constructed within a few years after a president leaves office. Most of the time cities clamor to be home to a presidential library. However, that was not the case with Nixon. There had been attempts over the years to find a home for a future Nixon library but because of the association with Watergate no city seemed to want it.

That finally changed. On July 19, 1990, the Richard Nixon Library and Birthplace opened in Yorba Linda, California, by the small house where he was born.

Nixon's library is a little different from other presidential libraries. Only his pre- and post-presidential papers are stored there. Because of legal decisions relating to Watergate, his presidential papers are stored in a Maryland warehouse operated by the National Archives and Records Administration (NARA). In addition, it is privately run, while other modern presidential libraries are operated by the NARA. In spite of those odd distinctions, the Yorba Linda complex is regarded as Richard Nixon's official presidential library.

Joining Nixon for the library dedication was a slew of important people including President George H.W. Bush, and former presidents Ford and Reagan. In a live television interview, newscaster Tom Brokaw asked Nixon if he ever thought the day would come when he had his own presidential library. Nixon honestly replied,

> Oh no, I really didn't. I remember, after I was very ill— you recall in 1974 I almost died because of an operation—I was pretty discouraged and Pat, my wife,

came in to see me. She said, 'Your girls are going to build that library for you.' I think perhaps without that encouragement we would never have done it.[16]

In 1991 the Nixons moved one more time, to a smaller home in a New Jersey community called Park Ridge. The once shunned former president continued to make public and television appearances discussing foreign affairs and urging the United States to aid Russia in its difficult change from a communist to a free enterprise economic system. After Democrat Bill Clinton was elected president in 1992, he invited Nixon to the

This re-creation of one of Nixon's favorite rooms in the White House, the Lincoln Sitting Room, is one of many exhibits at the Richard Nixon Library and Birthplace in Yorba Linda, California.

White House to ask advice about how to diplomatically deal with Russia. Nixon had morphed from a disgraced ex-president to a respected senior statesman.

On June 22, 1993, Pat Nixon died. At her funeral, the former president was visually shaken and teary-eyed. He and Pat had been married for fifty-three years. It was a major shock to Nixon to lose his wife. Still, he remained active, continuing to speak in public and even making a trip to Russia. Then on April 18, 1994, Nixon suffered a stroke. He died on April 22.

Both Nixons are buried on the grounds of Richard Nixon Library and Birthplace. At the thirty-seventh president's funeral, President Clinton proclaimed of Nixon, "He came to the presidency at a time in our history when Americans were tempted to say we had had enough of the world. Instead, he knew we had to reach out to old friends and old enemies alike. He would not allow America to quit the world."[17]

Implying that Nixon had suffered sufficiently for Watergate, Clinton stressed that it was time for people to move past the scandal. Clinton announced,

> Today is a day for his family, his friends, and his nation to remember President Nixon's life in totality. To them, let us say: may the day of judging President Nixon on anything less than his entire life and career come to a close. May we heed his call to maintain the will and the wisdom to build on America's greatest gift, its freedom, and to lead a world full of difficulty to the just and lasting peace he dreamed of.[18]

9

LEGACY

Regardless of President Clinton's request at Nixon's funeral, the majority of Americans still judge Richard Nixon primarily on one issue: Watergate. His former opponent during the 1972 presidential election, George McGovern, said of Nixon in 1997, "He'll be remembered as the only man that was forced to resign the presidency. There's no breaking that. It's just a historic fact."[1]

The year 1997 marked the twenty-fifth anniversary of the Watergate break-in. The year 2002 marked its thirtieth anniversary. Journalists and historians used the occasions to analyze the affair and what it meant to both Richard Nixon's legacy and the nation in general.

One journalist, Bill Schneider, recalled how during the years when Dwight Eisenhower and John F.

Kennedy were president the majority of Americans had faith in the government to be honest and do what's right. After all, the government had played major roles in both helping the nation recover from the Great Depression and leading the Allies to victory in World War II. And when Eisenhower and Kennedy were president, the federal government took an active part enacting social legislation during the civil rights movement.

But during the Vietnam War Americans lost confidence in the government. One reason was because they did not feel the government was being completely honest with the public regarding the course the war was taking.

Then came Nixon and Watergate. According to Bill Schneider, "Watergate turned an erosion of public confidence into a collapse."[2] Schneider added that in the years since Watergate, "Americans have come to believe the worst about government, politics and politicians."[3]

The legacy of the Watergate scandal still affects politics today. Republican President Ronald Reagan's administration (1981–1989) was investigated for numerous scandals, ranging from the serious to the trivial. The same was true of Democratic President Bill Clinton's two terms (1993–2001), which seemed to be filled with one scandal after another. One, which would lead down a long, winding road to impeachment, originally concerned a land purchase which had taken place over ten years before Clinton had even become president. Clinton survived impeachment, but everything he did was under scrutiny. The slightest error in judgment was seen as a reason for a major investigation. Political scholar Thomas Mann noted, "We now criminalize what in the old days would have been normal political give-and-take."[4]

Many Democrats interpreted the constant hounding of Clinton, including the impeachment, as a direct result of the Nixon scandal. To them, the Republicans wanted revenge for Watergate, especially because many liberals enthusiastically attacked Nixon during the Watergate years. To many Republicans, liberals wanted to attack Nixon without waiting to hear the full truth. The Clinton years were the time to give them a taste of their own medicine. Regardless of whether that claim is totally true, the fact that it was even brought up is a reflection of the staying power of Watergate.

Nixon's legacy was affected by his actions even after he died. The official papers of all presidents are kept private for some time after they have left office. Included are any private tape recordings a president may have made. For the sake of history, these papers and tapes are released to the public. But for reasons of national security, they are released little by little over a number of years.

Many of Nixon's papers and tapes which have been made public since his death have not been flattering. Some of the most disturbing comments heard by Nixon on some of the tapes seem to indicate he was anti-Semitic, or bigoted against Jews. For example, in tapes released in 1997 Nixon singled out Jews who contributed to the Democratic party and said they should have their income tax returns audited. In especially shocking tapes released in 2002, Nixon and a greatly admired minister, Reverend Billy Graham, both were caught making anti-Jewish remarks.

In one 1972 tape, Nixon implies that the American media are controlled by a Jewish conspiracy. Graham responds, "This stranglehold has got to be broken or this country's going down the drain."

Nixon replies, "You believe that?"

Graham answers, "Yes, sir."

Nixon agrees, "Oh boy. So do I. I can't ever say that but I believe it."

Graham then advises Nixon, "No, but if you get elected a second time, then we might be able to do something."[5]

Americans were shocked to hear those comments. Graham had always publicly spoken of his great respect for the Jews. And while it had been rumored for some time that Nixon personally held anti-Jewish views, he had many Jews on his staff while president. Herb Stein and Henry Kissinger were Jewish. So was William Safire, one of his top speech writers, and one of his best friends, Walter Annenberg. In addition, Nixon was thanked in 1973 by many Jews for sending weapons to Israel. The arms helped Israel win a war at the time against its Arab neighbors.

Both Graham's and Nixon's private conversation seemed to contradict their public behavior. Shortly after the tapes were made public, Graham personally apologized for his comments, saying they do not reflect his views. Some of Nixon's friends were his biggest defenders. In 1997, his former advisor Herb Stein said, "Certainly I can testify he was not anti-Semitic. He had a lot of Jewish advisors. He had a lot of Jewish friends who got along with him all very well. And he was one of Israel's greatest friends."[6]

Another disturbing topic which came to light as a result of released tapes was the way Nixon seemed to be uncaring about potential victims of the Vietnam War. In one tape, Henry Kissinger and Nixon discuss possible methods of broadening the war effort. Nixon says, "I'd rather use the nuclear bomb." Kissinger answers that that would be a dangerous idea. Nixon responds, "I just want you to think big."[7]

A historian named Stanley Karnow who has written much about the Vietnam War, said he highly doubts Nixon would really have used an atomic bomb. Karnow stated, "Just because he said it doesn't mean it was really an option."[8]

On the positive side, Nixon is still highly regarded for his work in foreign policy. When asked to name Nixon's greatest achievement, his former secretary of state William Rogers answered, "I think probably what will be his legacy in part that he contributed to world peace. What he did in connection with Communist

China and at the same time with the Soviet Union contributed to world peace."[9]

Because of conflicts over alleged human rights violations in China, the United States and the great Asian country have not always had a smooth relationship since Nixon's 1972 visit. But overall, the two powerful countries have worked together. On September 19, 2000, the United States Senate approved by a vote of 83 to 15 normal trade status for China. It was a historic decision, opening China up to perhaps billions of dollars for American businesses. President Clinton said, "It represents the most significant opportunity that we have had to create positive change in China since the 1970s, when President Nixon first went there and later in the decade when President Carter normalized relations."[10]

While liberals were always quick to criticize Nixon, it might be surprising that some of the positive elements of Nixon's legacy have been embraced by the same liberals. One is the founding of the Environmental Protection Agency. Another is Title IX. A news correspondent named Erin Hayes wrote in 1999,

> Since President Richard Nixon signed Title IX into law 27 years ago, a new generation of female athletes have changed sports in America. If you want to know what Title IX has accomplished, just watch the U.S. Women's soccer team, winner of the 1996 Olympics. They are babies who benefited from a girls' sports system in America that has gained a lot of ground since being kicked into gear by the law.[11]

In the years since Nixon resigned, many Americans including historians have lessened their anger at Gerald

Ford's pardon of Nixon. Many have accepted it as the right thing to do at the time. This was confirmed in a way when in 2001 the John F. Kennedy Library and Foundation awarded Ford one of its prestigious John F. Kennedy Profiles in Courage awards. While presenting Ford the award, President Kennedy's daughter Caroline Kennedy Schlossberg announced, "As President, he made the controversial decision of conscience to pardon former President Nixon and end the national trauma of Watergate. In doing so, he placed his love of country ahead of his own political future."[12]

So how should Richard Nixon be ranked among American presidents? Former Nixon advisor Herb Stein admitted,

> I think he should remembered as a man who achieved a great deal both in his personal life and in his career as president, but who made some bad mistakes and who in the end paid for those mistakes. If you were to take away Watergate, he would be remembered as a very good president. So I think he was a very good but flawed president.[13]

On the other hand, most historians give Nixon poor marks as president. In four surveys of historians taken in 1981, 1982 (when two were taken), and 1996, Nixon was ranked as one of the worst, in the category "failure." Two surveys of historians taken in 1997 and 2000 rank him a bit higher, but still fairly low. Interestingly, one of those was taken of mostly conservative Republicans by a group called the Intercollegiate Studies Institute. These conservatives ranked Democrats

Woodrow Wilson, John F. Kennedy, Lyndon Johnson, Jimmy Carter, and Bill Clinton among the worst and ranked conservative Rebublican Ronald Reagan as the fifth best. Still, they rated Nixon as "below average." Nixon's best showing was in a poll of historians taken by the public affairs cable network CSPAN in 2000. Nixon was ranked twenty-fifth out of forty-two presidents.[14]

Of course, many who lived through Watergate still carry personal angry feelings towards Nixon. A fresh viewpoint of Nixon's legacy has come from young adults born since Nixon's resignation. One, a news correspondent named Rebecca Howland who was born the year Nixon resigned, wrote that she sees Nixon's legacy as a mixture of good and bad. She said,

> To my generation, Nixon may not be remembered solely as a villain—our judgment is not impaired by a sense of betrayal or loss. And with the vantage point of history, perhaps, for us, Nixon can be—as he has become for many older Americans now that he is dead—both Watergate and China.[15]

CHRONOLOGY

1913—Born on January 9 in Yorba Linda, California.

1922—Moves with family to East Whittier, California.

1925—Lives with aunt in Lindsay, California.

1930—Attends Whittier College.
–1934

1934—Attends law school at Duke University.
–1937

1937—Practices law in Whittier.

1940—Marries Patricia (Pat) Ryan.

1942—Serves in U.S. Navy during World War II.
–1945

1946—Elected to U.S. House of Representatives; daughter Patricia (Tricia) born.

1948—Reelected to House of Representatives; daughter Julie born.

1948—As member of the House Committee on
–1949　UnAmerican Activities (HUAC) becomes deeply involved in Alger Hiss case.

1950—Elected to U.S. Senate.

1952—"Fund" ("Checkers") speech; elected vice-president of the United States under President Dwight D. Eisenhower.

1955—Takes over presidential duties when Eisenhower suffers heart attack.

1956—Reelected vice-president under Eisenhower.

1958—Attacked by mobs in Venezuela.

1959—"Kitchen debate" in Moscow with Soviet Union leader Nikita Khrushchev.

1960—Loses presidential election to John F. Kennedy.

1962—Loses race for governor of California.

1962—Works in private law practice.
–1968

1968—Elected president of the United States.

1969—Begins withdrawal of troops from Vietnam; "Silent Majority" speech.

1970—Sends United States troops into Cambodia, then withdraws them as promised; Kent State killings; secretly meets with student protesters in Washington; establishes Environmental Protection Agency (EPA) and Occupational Safety and Health Administration (OSHA).

1971—Enacts wage and price controls; Pentagon Papers published; "plumbers" group formed by White House staff.

1972—Major trips to China and Soviet Union; Watergate break-in; reelected president by huge margin.

1973—Cease-fire declared in Vietnam and United States fighting forces withdrawn; Watergate burglars plead or are found guilty; U.S. Senate begins holding hearings; Vice-President Agnew resigns; "Saturday Night Massacre" on October 20; House Judiciary Committee introduces twenty-one bills of impeachment.

1974—House Judiciary Committee recommends impeachment; resigns the presidency on August 9; pardoned by President Gerald Ford on September 8.

1979—First official trip to White House since resignation.

1990—Richard Nixon Library and Birthplace opens.

1993—Wife, Pat, dies on June 22.

1994—Dies on April 22.

DID YOU KNOW?

Trivia from the President's lifetime

Did you know that in the 1910s men started wearing wristwatches for the first time? Before that they carried pocket watches, since wristwatches were thought to be women's wear because they seemed similar to bracelets.

Did you know that in the 1920s anything considered to be excellent was called the cat's meow, the cat's whiskers, and sometimes the cat's pajamas?

Did you know that in the 1930s supermarkets first became popular? One store advertised, "You don't carry a cumbersome basket. You roll a carriage."

Did you know that in the 1940s fashionable teenage boys wore zoot suits? These consisted of baggy jackets with wide lapels; broad, padded shoulders; pants with high waists, cut full in the thigh, then tapered to a tight fit around the ankle; a wide-brimmed fedora hat; and a long, curving key chain.

Did you know that the biggest television program for children in the early 1950s was *The Howdy Doody Show*, starring a man named Buffalo Bob Smith and a freckle-faced marionette named Howdy Doody?

Did you know that the world's first theme park, *Disneyland*, opened near Nixon's birthplace in Anaheim, California, in 1955 on land which had once been occupied by orange groves and walnut trees?

Did you know that some of the most popular dances of the early 1960s had names like the mashed potato, the swim, the monkey, the jerk, and the most popular of all, the twist?

Did you know that in the early 1970s young people hung beaded curtains in the doorways in their homes as decorations?

Did you know in the mid–1970s, one of the most popular men's fashion fads was the leisure suit? It commonly consisted of a polyester jacket and matching flared pants, and a polyester shirt, usually with a loud pattern of stripes or polka-dots.

CHAPTER NOTES

Chapter 1. Breaking Down the Wall

1. Personal interview with William Rogers, January 27, 1997.
2. Ibid.
3. "Now, in Living Color from China," *Time*, February 28, 1972, p. 11.
4. Personal interview with George McGovern, February 10, 1997.
5. "World's Greatest Monuments," *InterActual Technologies, Inc.*, Mountain View, Calif. CD-ROM.
6. "Nixon in China: The First Steps of a Long March," *Newsweek*, March 6, 1972, p. 16.
7. Personal interview with William Rogers, January 27, 1997.

Chapter 2. I Want to Work on the Railroad

1. Personal interview with Scott Curtis, Margaret Herrick Library, Academy of Motion Picture Arts and Sciences, Los Angeles, November 18, 1996.
2. Transcript of birthplace narration audiotape, undated, Richard Nixon Library and Birthplace, Yorba Linda, Calif.
3. Jonathan Aitken, *Nixon: A Life* (Washington, D.C.: Regnery Publishing, Inc., 1993), p. 19.
4. Roger Morris, *Richard Milhous Nixon: The Rise of an American Politician* (New York: Henry Holt and Company, 1990), p. 59.
5. Transcript of birthplace narration audiotape.
6. Ibid.
7. Ibid.
8. Ibid.
9. *Biography*, television series, "Richard Nixon" episode, ABC News in association with Arts and Entertainment Network, executive producer Lisa Zeff, 1996.
10. Morris, p. 84.
11. Ibid.
12. Ibid.
13. *American Experience*, "Nixon," WGBH Educational Foundation with Thames Television, executive producer Judy Crichton, 1990.
14. Aitken, p. 29.
15. *The Real Richard Nixon*, "Early Years," videotape series, Central Park Media Corporation, Raiford Communications, 1994, 1995.
16. Richard Nixon, *RN: The Memoirs of Richard Nixon* (New York: Grosset & Dunlap, 1978), p. 15.
17. Aitken, p. 31.

Chapter 3. Marriage, War, and No Dancing

1. Richard Nixon, *RN: The Memoirs of Richard Nixon* (New York: Grosset & Dunlap, 1978), pp. 19–20.

2. Roger Morris, *Richard Milhous Nixon: The Rise of an American Politician* (New York: Henry Holt and Company, 1990), p. 142.

3. Ibid., p. 147.

4. Ibid., p. 157.

5. Jonathan Aitken, *Nixon: A Life* (Washington, D.C.: Regnery Publishing, Inc., 1993), p. 44.

6. Allan Nevins and Henry Steele Commager, *A Pocket History of the United States* (New York: Pocket Books, 1981), p. 416.

7. *The Real Richard Nixon*, "Early Years," videotape series, Central Park Media Corporation, Raiford Communications, Inc., 1994, 1995.

8. Aitken, p. 63.

9. *The Real Richard Nixon*, "Pat," videotape series.

10. Julie Nixon Eisenhower, *Pat Nixon: The Untold Story* (New York: Simon & Schuster, 1986), p. 34.

11. Stephen E. Ambrose, *Nixon: The Education of a Politician, 1913–1962*, vol. 1 (New York: Simon & Schuster, 1987), p. 104.

12. Nixon, p. 27.

Chapter 4. The Red Fighter

1. Richard Nixon, *RN: The Memoirs of Richard Nixon* (New York: Grosset & Dunlap, 1978), p. 34.

2. Tom Wicker, *One of Us: Richard Nixon and the American Dream* (New York: Random House, 1991, 1995), pp. 39–40.

3. Stephen E. Ambrose, *Nixon: The Education of a Politician, 1913–1962* (New York: Simon & Schuster, 1987), p. 132.

4. Wicker, p. 46.

5. *American Experience*, "Nixon," WGBH Educational Foundation with Thames Television, executive producer Judy Crichton, 1990.

6. Ibid.

7. Christopher Matthews, *Kennedy & Nixon: The Rivalry That Shaped Postwar America* (New York: Simon & Schuster, 1996), p. 51.

8. *Dateline NBC*, "Friends & Rivals," producer Tim Liehlinger, 1996.

9. Ambrose, p. 184.

10. Jonathan Aitken, *Nixon: A Life* (Washington, D.C.: Regnery Publishing, Inc., 1993), p. 174.

11. Aitken, p. 187.

12. Fawn M. Brodie, *Richard Nixon: The Shaping of His Character* (New York: W. W. Norton & Company, 1981), p. 241.

13. Ibid., p. 242.

14. Ralph de Toledano, *One Man Alone: Richard Nixon* (New York: Funk & Wagnalls, 1969), p. 115.

Chapter 5. Ike, Dick, Checkers, and Jack

1. Ralph de Toledano, *One Man Alone: Richard Nixon* (New York: Funk & Wagnalls, 1969), p. 117.

2. Stephen E. Ambrose, *Nixon: The Education of a Politician, 1913–1962* (New York: Simon & Schuster, 1987), p. 267.

3. Paul F. Boller, Jr., *Presidential Campaigns* (New York: Oxford University Press, 1985), p. 283.

4. Ibid., pp. 283–284.

5. Richard Nixon, *RN: The Memoirs of Richard Nixon* (New York: Grosset & Dunlap, 1978), p. 10.

6. Ibid., p. 392.

7. Ibid.

8. Richard Nixon, *Six Crises* (Garden City, N.Y.: Doubleday & Company, Inc., 1962), p. 115.

9. William A. DeGregorio, *The Complete Book of U.S. Presidents* (New York: Wings Books, 1991), p. 587.

10. *Television*, television series, episode 4, Educational Broadcasting Corp., production of WNET (New York), KCET (Los Angeles), in association with Granada Television of England, 1988.

11. Tom Wicker, *One of Us: Richard Nixon and the American Dream* (New York: Random House, 1991, 1995), p. 100.

12. Ambrose, p. 290.

13. Ibid.

14. *Biography*, television series, "Richard Nixon" episode, ABC NEWS in association with Arts and Entertainment Network, executive producer Lisa Zeff, 1996.

15. Ambrose, p. 277.

16. David C. Whitney, *The American Presidents* (Garden City, N.Y.: Doubleday & Co., Inc., 1978), p. 433.

17. Nixon, *RN: The Memoirs of Richard Nixon*, pp. 152–153.

18. Nixon, *Six Crises*, p. 133.

19. Ibid., p. 235.

20. Ibid.

21. Nixon, *Six Crises*, p. 319.

22. *Class of the Twentieth Century*, television series, episode 6, CEL Communications, Inc. and Arts and Entertainment Network, 1991.

23. *Television*, episode 4.

24. Whitney, p. 433.

25. Ibid.

26. *American Experience*, "Nixon," WGBH Educational Foundation with Thames Television, executive producer Judy Crichton, 1990.

27. "California: Career's End," *Time*, November 16, 1962, p. 16.

Chapter 6. President, At Last

1. Tim Brooks and Earle Marsh, *The Complete Directory to Prime Time Network and Cable TV Shows* (New York: Ballantine Books, 1995), p. 517.

2. *American Experience*, "Nixon," WGBH Educational Foundation with Thames Television, executive producer Judy Crichton, 1990.

3. Ted Yanak and Pam Cornelison, *The Great American History Fact-Finder* (New York: Houghton Mifflin Company, 1993), p. 396.

4. *Inside Politics*, CNN, April 23, 1994.

5. David C. Whitney, *The American Presidents* (Garden City, N.Y.: Doubleday & Co., Inc., 1978), p. 433.

6. Ibid.

7. William Safire, *Before the Fall* (Garden City, N.Y.: Doubleday & Company, Inc., 1975), p. 136.

8. "Text of President Nixon's Address to Nation on U.S. Policy in the War in Vietnam," *New York Times*, November 4, 1969, p. 16.

9. Ibid.

10. *American Experience*, "Nixon."

11. Whitney, p. 363.

12. Jonathan Aitken, *Nixon: A Life* (Washington, D.C.: Regnery Publishing, Inc., 1993), p. 403.

13. Richard Nixon, *RN: The Memoirs of Richard Nixon* (New York: Grosset & Dunlap, 1978), p. 456.

14. William A. DeGregorio, *The Complete Book of U.S. Presidents* (New York: Wings Books, 1991), p. 595.

15. *American Experience*, "Nixon."

16. Julie Nixon Eisenhower, *Pat Nixon: The Untold Story* (New York: Simon & Schuster, 1986), p. 287.

17. Ibid., p. 288.

18. Ibid.

19. DeGregorio, p. 595.

20. Personal interview with William Rogers, January 27, 1997.

21. Tom Wicker, *One of Us: Richard Nixon and the American Dream* (New York: Random House, 1991, 1995), p. 510.

22. Personal interview with Herb Stein, January 16, 1997.

23. Ibid.

24. Kristina Lindgren, "The Voices," *Los Angeles Times*, Orange County edition, Nixon Library special section, July 17, 1990, p. 14.

25. *Biography*, television series, "Richard Nixon" episode, ABC NEWS in association with Arts and Entertainment Network, executive producer Lisa Zeff, 1996.

26. Henry Kissinger, *White House Years* (Boston: Little, Brown and Company, 1979), p. 730.

27. Clifton Daniel, ed., *Chronicle of the 20th Century* (Liberty, Mo.: JL International Publishing, 1992), p. 1047.

Chapter 7. The National Nightmare

1. *Biography*, television series, "Richard Nixon" episode, ABC NEWS in association with Arts and Entertainment Network, executive producer Lisa Zeff, 1996.

2. William A. DeGregorio, *The Complete Book of U.S. Presidents* (New York: Wings Books, 1991), p. 595.

3. Paul F. Boller, Jr., *Presidential Campaigns* (New York: Oxford University Press, 1985), p. 337.

4. David C. Whitney, *The American Presidents* (Garden City, N.Y.: Doubleday & Co., Inc., 1978), p. 433.

5. Personal interview with George McGovern, February 10, 1997.

6. DeGregorio, p. 596.

7. John J. Sirica, *To Set the Record Straight* (New York: W. W. Norton, 1979), pp. 97–98.

8. Stephen E. Ambrose, *Nixon: Ruin and Recovery, 1973–1990* (New York: Simon & Schuster, 1991), p. 231.

9. *Our World*, ABC News, executive producer Peter Kunhardt, 1986.

10. *Watergate: The Secret Story*, CBS, Inc., and Post/Newsweek Stations, executive producer Andrew Lack, 1992.

11. Ibid.

12. Clifton Daniel, ed., *Chronicle of the 20th Century* (Liberty, Mo.: JL International Publishing, 1992), p. 1081.

13. *The Real Richard Nixon*, "The Final Twenty-Eight Days," videotape series, Central Park Media Corporation, Raiford Communications, 1994, 1995.

14. Ibid.

15. Ibid.

16. Videotaped conversation exhibited at Richard Nixon Library and Birthplace, Yorba Linda, California.

17. Personal interview with Herb Stein, January 16, 1997.

18. *The Real Richard Nixon*, "The Final Twenty-Eight Days," videotape series.

19. Personal interview with Herb Stein, January 16, 1997.

20. Personal interview with George McGovern, February 10, 1997.

Chapter 8. The Fall and Rise of Richard Nixon

1. Richard Nixon, *In The Arena* (New York: Simon & Schuster, 1990), p. 14.

2. Ralph Keyes, *The Wit & Wisdom of Harry Truman* (New York: HarperCollins Publishers, 1995), p. 70.

3. Gerald R. Ford, *A Time To Heal* (New York: Harper & Row, Publishers, 1979), p. 178.

4. Nixon, p. 21.

5. Stephen E. Ambrose, *Nixon: Ruin and Recovery, 1973–1990* (New York: Simon & Schuster, 1991), p. 461.

6. Ford, pp. 178–179.

7. Robert Sam Anson, *Exile: The Unquiet Oblivion of Richard M. Nixon* (New York: Simon & Schuster, 1984), p. 88.

8. Ambrose, p. 502.

9. "Sir David Frost—a profile," British Broadcasting Co. Web site, <http://news.bbc.co.uk/1/hi/programmes/breakfast_with_frost/737846.stm> originally dated May 19, 2000, downloaded October 23, 2002.

10. "Press Room: Discovery Civilization Channel to Mark 30th Anniversary of Watergate Break-In With Premiere of Never-Before-Seen Footage From Historic David Frost Interviews With Richard Nixon," The New York Times in Television Web site, <http://www.nytco.com/subsites/nyttv/0603watergate.html> originally dated June 3, 2002, downloaded October 23, 2002.

11. Ibid.

12. "Nixon, Richard Milhous (1913)" The Oxford Dictionary of Quotations Web site, <http://www.xrefer.com/entry/249169> (Oxford University Press, 1999), downloaded October 23, 2002.

13. Ambrose, p. 512.

14. Ibid., p. 560.

15. Larry Martz, Thomas M. DeFrank, Howard Fineman, Martin Kasindorf, and Jonathan Alter, "The Road Back," *Newsweek*, May 19, 1986, p. 27.

16. NBC Nightly News telecast, July 19,1990, anchor Tom Brokaw.

17. "Funeral Services of President Nixon," Richard Nixon Library & Birthplace Foundation Web site, <http://www.nixonfoundation.org/Research_Center/Nixons/RichardNixonFuneral.html> downloaded October 23, 2002.

18. Ibid.

Chapter 9. Legacy

1. Personal interview with George McGovern, February 10, 1997.

2. Bill Schneider, "Cynicism Didn't Start With Watergate," Cable News Network Web site, <http://www.cnn.com/ALLPOLITICS/1997/gen/resources/watergate/trust.schneider/> originally dated June 17, 1997, downloaded October 18, 2002.

3. Ibid.

4. Brooks Jackson, "A Watergate Legacy: More Public Skepticism, Ambivalence," Cable News Network Web site, <http://www.cnn.com/

ALLPOLITICS/1997/gen/resources/watergate/watergate/jackson> originally dated June 17, 1997, downloaded October 18, 2002.

5. Darlene Superville, Associated Press, "Billy Graham apologizes for anti-Semitic remarks to Nixon," The Detroit News Web site, <http://www.detnews.com/2002/religion/0203/10/religion-430343.htm> originally dated March 2, 2002, downloaded October 24, 2002.

6. Personal interview with Herb Stein, January 16, 1997.

7. "Nixon, The A-Bomb, And Napalm," Columbia Broadcasting System Web site, <http://www.cbsnews.com/stories/2002/03/05/politics/printable502986.shtml> originally dated February 28, 2002, downloaded October 19, 2002.

8. Ibid.

9. Personal interview with William Rogers, January 27, 1997.

10. Jim Abrams, Associated Press, "China Trade Bill Approved," American Broadcasting Company Web site, <http://abcnews.go.com/sections/world/DailyNews/china000919.html> originally dated September 19, 2000, downloaded October 19, 2002.

11. Erin Hayes, "Leveling the Playing Field," American Broadcasting Company Web site, <http://abcnews.go.com/onair/CloserLook/wnt990617_hayes_story.html> originally dated June 17, 1999, downloaded October 19, 2002.

12. "President Gerald Ford and Congressman John Lewis Honored as Profiles in Courage," The John F. Kennedy Library and Foundation newsletter, Summer 2001, p. 16.

13. Personal interview with Herb Stein, January 16, 1997.

14. Meena Bose, "Presidential Ratings: Lessons and Liabilities," paper abstract prepared for delivery at the 2001 Annual Meeting of the American Political Science Association, San Francisco, August 30–September 2, 2001, <http://pro.harvard.edu/abstracts/023/023010BoseMeena0.htm> downloaded October 26, 2002.

15. Rebecca Howland, "Confessions of a Watergate Baby," American Broadcasting System Web site, <http://more.abcnews.go.com/sections/us/watergate/watergate_genx.html> originally dated 1997, downloaded October 19, 2002.

FURTHER READING

Dudley, Mark E. *United States vs. Nixon, 1974: Presidential Powers*. Brookfield, Conn.: Twenty-First Century Books, Inc., 1994.

Eisenhower, Julie Nixon. *Pat Nixon: The Untold Story*. New York: Simon & Schuster, 1986.

Hay, Jeff. Ed. *Richard M. Nixon*. Farmington Hills, Mich.: Gale Group, 2001.

Marquez, Heron. *Richard Nixon*. Minneapolis, Minn.: Lerner Publishing Group, 2002.

Nixon, Richard. *Six Crises*. Garden City, N.Y.: Doubleday & Company, Inc., 1962.

INTERNET ADDRESSES

The National Park Service, including the Vietnam War Memorial

<http://www.nps.gov>

The Richard Nixon Library and Birthplace

<http://www.nixonfoundation.org/index.shtml>

White House Historical Association

<http://www.whitehousehistory.org>

PLACES TO VISIT

California

Richard Nixon Library and Birthplace, Yorba Linda. (714) 993-3393. This is Richard Nixon's presidential library. It is filled with high-tech exhibits. Galleries cover Nixon's life, including his childhood, his years in Congress, the Alger Hiss case, China, the Vietnam War, and Watergate. One can also tour Nixon's birthplace and visit Richard and Pat Nixon's graves. Open year-round.

Michigan

Gerald Ford Presidential Museum, Grand Rapids. (616) 451-9263. This is former President Gerald Ford's official presidential museum. It includes exhibits about his pardon of Nixon. Open year-round.

Washington, D.C.

Vietnam Veterans Memorial. (202) 485-9875. The names of all those who died in the war are inscribed on a black granite V-shaped wall. Nearby are realistic, life-size statues of six anonymous servicepeople aiding a wounded soldier. Open year-round.

INDEX